The House
Built on the Sand

The House Built on the Sand

Tony Pearce

New Wine Press

New Wine Ministries
PO Box 17
Chichester
West Sussex
United Kingdom
PO19 2AW

ISBN 1-903725-70-4

Typeset by CRB Associates, Reepham, Norfolk
Cover design by CCD, www.ccdgroup.co.uk
Printed in Malta

Contents

The House
Built on the Sand

Two hundred years ago the fastest anyone could go anywhere in the world was the speed of a horse. The fastest you could send a message anywhere in the world was to give it to someone to carry it from A to B at the speed of a horse. It was the same in the time of Julius Caesar, Alexander the Great and back as far as we can look into history.

Today you can get to the other side of the world by jet plane in just over a day; you can speak by phone or communicate by email instantly with someone thousands of miles away. Technology is advancing so fast that today's most advanced computers, mobile phones and a host of other gadgets, will be out of date within a few years, if not months.

Two hundred years ago, as two thousand years ago, the majority of people never travelled far from the place they were born, and had little or no idea of other cultures and ideas. Most white people living in Europe had never seen a black person and most black people living in Africa had never seen a white person.

Today travel and communications mean that the world has become a global village and people of all races share living space, ideas, entertainment, sport, music and religion in a way our forefathers could never have imagined.

Two hundred years ago, as two thousand years ago, if you wanted to build, grow food, go to war or travel, you needed the sweat of human labour with the help of animals like the ox, the horse, the donkey and the camel to accomplish these things.

Today the discovery of coal, oil, gas and nuclear power, means that machines will do the back-breaking jobs that our ancestors had to do by human sweat with the help of animals. Trains, cars and planes will transport us in hours to places that previously it would have taken weeks, months or even years to get to.

The huge increase in travel has shrunk our world to a global village and the incredible developments of technology over the past hundred years have filled our shops and our homes with gadgets and machines that our forefathers had absolutely no concept of. In the prophecies of Daniel written some 2,500 years ago we find some amazing information relating this situation to the 'time of the end', the last days of this age before the event known in the Old Testament as the Day of the Lord and in the New Testament as the Second Coming of Christ.

> But you, Daniel, shut up the words, and seal the book until the time of
> the end; many shall run to and fro, and knowledge shall increase.
>
> (Daniel 12:4)

Go to an airport in a major world city and you will see people running to an fro about to take journeys across the globe. Switch on a computer and open up the Internet and you can tap into an almost infinite source of knowledge on whatever you want to know. We are all witnesses of the fulfilment of these words of Daniel.

All these developments open up many exciting possibilities which our ancestors could only have dreamed about. But there is a downside. Although the labours of the past were much harder and only capable of accomplishing a fraction of what modern machines can do, they had two great advantages. They had no negative impact on the environment. They were entirely renewable. People came and went, animals were strong for a while and then died, but whether they were in Europe or China or anywhere else they were able to reproduce and provide for the next generation to carry on living in the same way as their ancestors had done. Apart from deserts and high mountains, the basic resources for keeping society going were available wherever you lived in the world.

Today the resources needed to keep our wonderful world going are finite. They are found only in certain places, some of them, especially Middle Eastern oil, in very vulnerable places which right now are passing through a period of instability which could plunge the whole world into sudden chaos.

Journalists, politicians, scientists and religious figures commenting on our time generally assume that it is inevitable that the kind of dizzying progress we have seen in our time will continue indefinitely. There will be new forms of computers, mobile phones, cars and planes capable of doing ever more advanced things. Even if oil runs out we will develop some other means of generating power so we can keep the system going generation after generation.

There are 'prophets of doom' but generally they are dismissed as cranks who are marginal to society and deserve to be ignored and mocked. There are Hollywood movies like *Deep Impact* showing a comet hitting the earth or *The Day After Tomorrow* with its stunning visual effects of sudden weather changes plunging the world into a deep freeze. But generally the effect of these movies is to relegate the possibility of such things really happening to the realm of a Hollywood fantasy which does not need to be taken too seriously.

But you don't need to go into the realm of Hollywood fantasy to see that our society is built on shaky foundations. Modern technological society lines up with the well known words spoken by Jesus:

> 'Whoever hears these sayings of Mine, and does them, I will liken him to a wise man who built his house upon the rock: and the rain descended, the floods came, and the winds blew and beat on that house; and it did not fall, for it was founded on the rock. But everyone who hears these sayings of Mine, and does not do them, will be like a foolish man who built his house on the sand: and the rain descended, the floods came, and the winds blew and beat on that house; and it fell. And great was its fall.'

(Matthew 7:24–27)

Sooner or later the storm will come and this house will crash. What will happen to you and me then? In this book we will look at a number of reasons why we are living in a house built on the sand and what we can do about it.

The House of Saud

In March 2004 BBC2 broadcast a programme called *If the Lights Go Out*. It was a fictional documentary set in 2015 which featured a scenario in which Britain had become dependent on imported natural gas from Russia and Algeria for its energy supply. Terrorists blew up the main gas pipeline near St Petersburg causing a shutdown of electricity supply across Europe. The film showed what happened when the lights went out in London and stayed out for days – chaos, looting and terror.

January 2006 began with a crisis caused by Russia demanding a huge increase in charges to Ukraine for its gas supply and threatening to cut supplies if the price was not paid. Many saw this as Russia punishing Ukraine for its pro-Western policies. But the threat to turn off the gas supplies in the middle of winter did not just affect Ukraine. For a few days countries across Europe watched nervously as the crisis unfolded.

The deputy chairman of Gazprom, the giant Russian company that controls the flow of Russian gas to the West, came to London to reassure Britain that there would be no risk of disruption to British gas supplies. The very next day, temperatures in Moscow broke a fifty-year record, plunging to $-30°$C. Gas normally exported was diverted to the home front. Supplies to the West fell. Nervousness on this subject was increased by news reports that Gazprom is seeking to buy a controlling share in British Gas.

As huge price rises for gas supply are announced, the prospect of the source of this supply being in the hands of a power which once confronted the West during the Cold War is hardly reassuring. After all, Russian President Putin had once written a thesis saying that Russia could use its energy resources to regain its global power. Russia supplies a quarter of all the gas used in Europe and 90% of it flows through Ukraine. This supply is scheduled to increase when a giant pipeline now being built under the North Sea from Russia to Germany is completed. Britain will be at the end of the line for this gas which will become vital as our North Sea oil and gas decline.

The potential for a cut off of supplies of oil is even more alarming. In January 2006 Iran threatened to cut oil supplies if Europe continued to meddle in what it sees as its right to develop a nuclear programme. It has also threatened to block shipping through the Straits of Hormuz at the entrance of the Persian Gulf if its nuclear facilities are attacked. Every day, 15 million barrels of oil pass in tankers through these narrow Straits.

Commenting on this situation, Jeremy Leggett, a former oil man, wrote an article in *The Independent* (20/1/06) entitled, 'What they don't want you to know about the coming oil crisis'. He wrote:

> A spectre is haunting Europe – the spectre of an acute, civilisation-changing energy crisis ... We have allowed oil to become vital to virtually everything we do. Ninety per cent of all our transportation, whether by land, air or sea, is fuelled by oil. Ninety-five per cent of all goods in shops involve the use of oil. Ninety-five per cent of all our food products require oil use. Just to farm a single cow and deliver it to market requires six barrels of oil, enough to drive a car from New York to Los Angeles.
>
> The world consumes more than 80 million barrels of oil a day, 29 billion barrels a year, at the time of writing. This figure is rising fast, as it has done for decades. The almost universal expectation is that it will keep doing so for years to come. The US

government assumes that global demand will grow to around 120 million barrels a day, 43 billion barrels a year, by 2025. Few question the feasibility of this requirement, or the oil industry's ability to meet it. They should, because the oil industry won't come close to producing 120 million barrels a day; nor is there any prospect of the shortfall being taken up by gas. In other words, the most basic of the foundations of our assumptions of future economic wellbeing is rotten. Our society is in a state of collective denial that has no precedent in history, in terms of its scale and implications.

The modern industrial world has been built on the supply of energy keeping the electricity supply to our homes and work places running and fuelling our transport system which ensures that goods and people can move from place to place around the world. Without the energy sources – coal, oil, gas and nuclear power – the whole system crumbles.

Britain still has large deposits of coal, but most of the mines have been shut down and coal is being phased out as an energy source because of the pollution it causes. Nuclear power stations are nearing the end of their lives and plans to build new ones are being contested by the environmental lobby. If the decision is taken to build new nuclear power stations it will be many years before they are operational. North Sea oil and gas are running out. According to some projections it will not be long before Britain will begin to be dependent on other countries for its energy supply. Without that energy supply the system will grind to a halt.

In America that possibility is beginning to be considered by those who see the phenomenon known as 'Peak Oil' as the next big threat to the Western way of life. Peak Oil is the point at which oil production reaches a plateau before it declines, while demand for oil consumption continues to rise. Once worldwide demand for oil outpaces worldwide production of oil by a significant margin the price of oil will skyrocket, oil-dependent economies will crumble, and resource wars will explode.

Matthew Savinar has written an article on this subject on the Internet website http://www.lifeaftertheoilcrash.net. He writes:

> Civilization as we know it is coming to an end soon. This is not the wacky proclamation of a doomsday cult, apocalypse bible prophecy sect, or conspiracy theory society. Rather, it is the scientific conclusion of the best paid, most widely-respected geologists, physicists, and investment bankers in the world. These are rational, professional, conservative individuals who are absolutely terrified by a phenomenon known as global 'Peak Oil'.

When will this happen? According to Savinar, 'Some geologists expect 2005 to be the last year of the cheap-oil bonanza, while many estimates coming out of the oil industry indicate 'a seemingly unbridgeable supply-demand gap opening up after 2007', which will lead to major fuel shortages and increasingly severe blackouts beginning around 2008–2012.' Richard Heinberg, in his article 'Smoking Gun: The CIA's Interest in Peak Oil' expresses a similar view:

> Pessimists say the global peak may already have occurred in 2000; optimists say it won't come until 2025 or so. A growing consensus of petroleum geologists places this event in the mid-range period of 2006 to 2015.

Savinar dismisses alternatives to oil as sources of power for the current world system as fantasy. Green alternatives like solar, wind and wave power produce only a tiny fraction of the power now available through oil. In 2003 they produced less than one-sixth of one percent of the energy appetite of the USA. Hydrogen as an alternative to oil does not work either due to the huge costs of producing it and the vast problems of storing it. Nuclear energy is of limited use and is highly dangerous to the environment. Biofuels such as ethanol and biodiesel are no solution as growing enough rape, maize or sugar cane to produce the required amount of oil for the demands of a country like the USA or Great Britain would involve covering 97% of the land with crops to produce oil, which would not leave much for producing food! Moreover, he says there is no time to develop the huge infrastructure needed to switch from an oil-based industrial system to an alternative one. Nor is there the political will or the financial capability.

Savinar sees an inevitable collapse of the US economy coming, which will drag down the rest of the world. He writes:

> The US has built its entire infrastructure and way of life under the assumption oil would always be cheap and plentiful. Since that is no longer the case, the US economy is in even more trouble than the economies of other first world nations such as the UK, Germany, Spain, and France. Each of these countries has mass transit, light rail, and/or renewable energy infrastructures that put the US to shame. Thus, even in the best-case scenario, we're looking at a financial meltdown and a collapse of the value of US dollar so severe that the Great Depression will look like the 'good ole days.' The end of cheap oil also means the elimination of Great Depression era social programs such as Social Security and Medicare.
>
> As the US economy begins to disintegrate, massive civil unrest may break out as the various factions of the divided American citizenry seek to blame the economic situation on whoever their favourite scapegoat is. Liberals and blue-states (Democrats) will blame 'Bush, Big-Oil and the Hard Right Neocons' while conservatives and red-staters (Republicans) will blame 'Bin-Laden, Big-Government, and the Extreme Left Environmentalists.' Both groups will likely gravitate to and rally around reactionary political demagogues who promise to bring back the good days by eliminating whatever domestic or foreign groups they have decided are at fault for the economic and geopolitical unravelling. Put simply, the end of oil may result in the end of America as we know it.
>
> As the driver of the world's economy, the demise of the US will take down other industrialized countries such as those mentioned above. The financial dislocations wrought by the coming oil

shocks could set the stage for a series of destabilizing resource wars and 'currency insurgencies', in much the same way Germany's financial meltdown during the Weimar Republic of the 1920s set the stage for the rise of Third Reich in the 1930s and World War II in the 1940s.

It is not just in America that this scenario is beginning to be taken seriously. In October 2005, *The Times* acknowledged that the world's wealth may soon evaporate as we enter a technological and economic 'Dark Age'. In an article entitled 'Waiting for the Lights to Go Out' *The Times* reporter Bryan Appleyard wrote the following:

> Oil is running out; the climate is changing at a potentially catastrophic rate; wars over scarce resources are brewing; finally, most shocking of all, we don't seem to have any ideas about how to fix any of these things. Almost daily, new evidence is emerging that progress can no longer be taken for granted, that a new Dark Age is lying in wait for ourselves and our children. Growth may be coming to an end. Since our entire financial order – interest rates, pension funds, insurance, stock markets – is predicated on growth, the social and economic consequences may be cataclysmic.

In 2005 the world consumed about 84 million barrels of oil a day. America alone guzzled about 20.8 million barrels a day. A disruption anywhere could cause market panic and spiralling prices. Texas oil analyst Matt Simmons has written a book *Twilight in the Desert*, which warns that the skyrocketing price of oil could plunge the world into war. One spark which could ignite this fire is the tension over Iran's nuclear programme which is causing worry about possible disruptions of the supply of oil from the Middle East. Nigeria is another unstable source of oil, with insurgents attacking oil installations and oil companies withdrawing their workers. At the time of writing (January 2006), news reports have featured the possibility of losing oil supply from both Nigeria and Iran.

All of this focuses attention on the Middle East, where 70% of global proven reserves of oil are to be found. Saudi Arabia has the world's largest reserves with 264.2 billion barrels of proven oil reserves (25% of the world total). Oil from this area is the easiest to extract and export. Recent finds of oil in the Caspian Sea area and in Central Asia are not as great as was originally hoped and these areas are landlocked so getting the oil out involves building pipelines through such unstable regions as Afghanistan to the south or the Caucasus region to the west. The vulnerability of pipelines to terrorism has been shown by the frequent attacks mounted by insurgents in Iraq.

Production of oil is in decline in more than fifty oil-producing nations, including the USA and Britain. Discoveries of large oil fields are decreasing year by year, while the demand for oil is constantly increasing. In particular, China and India are already having a major impact on both oil resources and the environment on account of their huge populations and growing numbers of people prospering as a result of economic development. By the end of 2005 China had become the second largest consumer, using more than 20% of global oil supplies, and leading to an increase in demand. Just one in 1,000 people wanting to own a car in China means another million cars on the roads.

There have been large finds of oil in Russia with deep wells sunk in Siberia. However, Russia could well prove an unreliable source of supply. A recently released CIA document reveals that during the 1980s the Reagan Administration persuaded the Saudis to flood the world with cheap oil in order to undercut Russian oil and bankrupt the economy of the USSR. If the tables were turned and America found itself in need of extra oil, is it likely that Russia would come to the rescue? Or would Russia, which is increasingly pursuing a foreign policy which is competing with America and the West, use this as a means to break America's power?

This brings us back to the Middle East, which must remain the main source of oil supply for the world in the foreseeable future. All the main oil-producing countries of the Middle East, Saudi Arabia, Iraq and Iran, are Islamic. Iran is already in the hands of

Islamic extremists who hate the West and Saudi Arabia and Iraq
are threatened by them. Osama Bin Laden and the jihadis have
said many times that their war against the West is not only a
religious war but an economic war. Bin Laden began his jihad
fighting the Russians in Afghanistan with the support of the
Americans who saw him as an ally in the fight against Soviet
Communism. Bin Laden's strategy was simple and devastating:
'We bled the Russians to the point of bankruptcy. So if we were
able to do it to them, we can now do it to the Americans, and the
best way to do it is to go after their Achilles heel and attack oil.'

The 2005 elections in Iran brought to power the most extreme
faction of the Islamic Revolution. Iran's President Ahmadinejad
has called for the destruction of the state of Israel and for the
elimination of Christianity in the country. Ahmadinejad made
clear his global intentions just after his election victory: 'We did
not carry out the Islamist revolution in order to introduce
democracy. Our revolution seeks to achieve worldwide power.
The new Islamic revolution will cut out the roots of injustice
throughout the world. The era of the godless regime, tyranny and
injustice has come to an end. The wave of the Islamist revolution
will soon reach the entire world.' Ahmadinejad believes that the
world is heading for a clash of civilisations in which Islam is
the only credible alternative to Western domination. And he is
convinced that Islam can and will win.

Part of Ahmadinejad's conviction comes from his belief in the
second coming of the 12th Imam. According to the Shiite version of
Islam the 12th descendant of Muhammad, known as the 12th Imam
or the Mahdi, went into hiding in 941. Shiites believe he will
reappear when the world has become full of oppression and
tyranny. They believe that he is hidden in the Jamkaran well in
Iran, which is a place of pilgrimage for believers who drop their
requests for help into the well in the hope that the Imam will read
them and come to their aid. Ahmadinejad has said, 'Our revolution's main mission is to pave the way for the reappearance of the
12th Imam, the Mahdi. We should define our economic, cultural
and political policies on the policy of the Imam Mahdi's return.'

Ahmadinejad connects this belief with the desire to create a strong Iran capable of standing against its enemies and projecting its power into the region. The development of Iran's nuclear industry is seen as a vital part of this programme. Iran is building a nuclear power station with help from the Russians at Busheir in the south of the country. The international community is concerned that this will be used to manufacture nuclear weapons. As Iran has missiles capable of reaching Israel and beyond, this is a severe threat to the stability of the region. The hard-line Islamic regime in Iran has made no secret of its desire to annihilate the Jewish state. The leaders of Iran have stated that any attack on their nuclear facilities by Israel or the USA would 'open the gates of hell'.

To the west of Iran lies Iraq, a country which has about 11% of the world's oil reserves. Opponents of the war in Iraq accused the Bush administration of going to war for the world's last remaining significant deposits of oil. If this was the motivation it is by no means certain that it will achieve the desired result. Since the end of the invasion of Iraq and the toppling of Saddam's regime, there have been close to 300 attacks on pipelines, refineries, and other facilities in Iraq. There have also been attacks on oil installations in many other parts of the world, including Chechnya, Pakistan, India, Russia, Azerbaijan, and Nigeria. The impact of those attacks amounts to about 1 million barrels a day that have been taken off the market as a result of sabotage. If these million barrels a day had reached the market, oil prices would be at least $20 a barrel lower. This shows that the jihadis, using very simple tactics, have been very successful in driving up oil prices significantly, taking advantage of a very tight market.

A report released by the Royal Institute of International Affairs in September 2004 warned of the possibility that Iraq could splinter into civil war and destabilize the whole region if the interim government, US forces and United Nations fail to hold the ring among factions struggling for power. 'Even if U.S. forces try to hold out and prop up the central authority in Iraq, it may still lose control,' the report said. In the worst case, instability in Iraq would suck in its neighbours, Iran, Turkey, Syria, Jordan and Saudi Arabia causing a regional upheaval which the report said would be 'beyond U.S. or multinational control'.

To the south-west of Iraq lies Saudi Arabia. Saudi Arabia is by far the most important oil-producing nation in the world. The world looks to Saudi Arabia to meet any shortfalls in oil caused by crises in other oil-producing countries. According to the article already quoted by Jeremy Leggett in *The Independent*, Saudi Arabia may not be as well able to meet future needs as the rest of the world is hoping. The Saudis are already pumping at or near their peak and reports by Saudi engineers show that pressure is dropping in Saudi oilfields. The four biggest fields (Ghawar, Safaniyah, Hanifa, and Khafji) are all more than fifty years old, having produced almost all Saudi oil in the past half-century. These days they have to be kept flowing largely by injection of water. Oil expert Matthew Simmons says: 'We could be on the verge of seeing a collapse of 30 or 40 per cent of their production in the imminent future. And imminent means some time in the next three to five years – but it could even be tomorrow.' In February 2005, Simmons speculated that the Saudis may have damaged their giant oilfields by over-producing them in the past: a geological phenomenon known as 'rate sensitivity'. In oilfields where the oil is pumped too hard, the structure of the oil reservoir can be impaired. 'If Saudi Arabia has damaged its fields, accidentally or not,' Simmons said, 'then we may already have passed peak oil.'

Even this gloomy view of the future of the Saudi oil industry depends on the political situation in Saudi Arabia remaining stable. The oil industry relies on the expertise of its foreign employees who have benefited for years from the high salaries with no income tax and luxurious accommodation available. These workers will not stay in Saudi Arabia unless the government takes significant steps to defend them. Western interests also depend on the goodwill of the Saudi royal family, who are themselves the object of hatred by the Islamists. The war on terror is also being played out in Saudi Arabia and the consequence of losing it would be Bin Laden or his followers with the West's oil supplies in their hands.

Newsweek (28/6/04) carried a report on a visit to Saudi Arabia by Fareed Zakaria entitled 'Is Saudi Arabia doomed?' His answer to this question is not encouraging. 'A secret government poll showed that 49% of the population supports Osama Bin Laden's ideas ... 25% of the Saudi GDP goes towards the support of the royal family and its patronage networks.' While Saudi princes live in fantastic luxury, large parts of Riyadh are decaying. Alongside the shacks inhabited by the poor stand magnificent palaces. Zakaria writes:

> The complex which totals hundreds of acres is a mile-long high-walled compound of buildings, cloistered by hundreds of leafy trees rising out of the desert ... The palace in Jeddah is a waterfront estate, also vast and walled with two exquisitely carved Spanish style towers rising out of it, dwarfing virtually everything in the city. An Arab diplomat who has been to one of the palaces recalls that inside the compound the roads are paved with Italian marble.

He questioned this to a government official who said, 'Well the French have Versailles.' Zakaria commented: 'I could not help but note, "Yes, and then they had a revolution."'

If revolution comes to Saudi Arabia it is not likely to be won by democrats pushing for a just and peaceful republic to replace the corrupt autocratic rule of the House of Saud. It is likely to be won by supporters of Islamic radicalism dedicated to driving out the Western influences which they believe are polluting the land holy to Allah. In particular the presence of about 5,000 US troops in Saudi Arabia, home to Islam's two holiest sites, is al-Qaeda's bitterest grievance against America – both because they are offended by having 'infidel troops' in what Muslims regard as the holy land of Saudi Arabia and because the US presence makes it harder for them to topple the Saudi monarchy.

These radicals see the occupying forces as a 'Crusader–Zionist alliance' bent on dividing and ruling the Arab world in order to 'serve the Jews' petty state (i.e. Israel) and divert attention from its occupation of Jerusalem.' In response they call on all Muslims to kill Americans:

> The ruling to kill the Americans and their allies – civilians and military – is an individual duty for every Muslim who can do it in any country in which it is possible to do it, in order to liberate the al-Aqsa Mosque [in Jerusalem] and the holy mosque [in Mecca] from their grip, and in order for their armies to move out of all the lands of Islam, defeated and unable to threaten any Muslim. This is in accordance with the words of Almighty Allah: 'And fight the pagans all together as they fight you all together,' and 'Fight them until there is no more tumult or oppression, and there prevail justice and faith in Allah.'

On February 22nd 2006 two al-Qaeda car bombers attempted an attack on Saudi Arabia's largest oil complex at Abqaiq. This facility, which processes 60 percent of Saudi Arabia's 9.5 million barrels per day oil production, is located about 8 miles from Ras Tanura (on the Persian Gulf), the largest oil terminal in the world and the primary outlet of Saudi oil exports. Had the attack been successful, oil prices would have likely broken all records possibly causing a worldwide economic crisis. A website linked to al-Qaeda claimed responsibility and vowed to launch similar operations against Saudi oil installations, which it believes are surrendering the kingdom energy's wealth to 'infidels' to help sustain their economy. This is in line with Bin Laden's call, reiterated by his deputy, Ayman al-Zawahiri, to target the Arab world's oil industry.

But it is not just al Qaeda and its supporters who are stirring up hatred against Americans and their allies in Saudi Arabia. Government sponsored mosques and TV stations frequently air preachers making the same claims and demands. These preachers speak of a 'big explosion coming', justify suicide terrorism 'if it causes great damage to the enemy' and prophesy the coming collapse of America.

Saudi professor Nasser Bin Suleiman Al-Omar, who runs a large Islamic Internet website, appeared on the United Arab Emirates TV station, Al-Majd, on June 13, 2004, to discuss the approaching collapse of the US and the growing strength of Muslims within the US:

> America is collapsing from within. Islam is advancing according to a steady plan, to the point that tens of thousands of Muslims have joined the American army and Islam is the second largest religion in America. Today, America is defeated. I have no doubt, not even for a minute, that America is on its way to destruction.[1]

Saudi Arabia is the heartland of Islam from where Muhammad embarked on his mission to conquer the world for Islam. It has used the incredible wealth generated by its oil industry to spread Islam throughout the world. The world vision of Islam from the days of its inception is to bring the world into subjection to Allah as defined in the Koran. Muhammad's mission was universal, with the aim of not only preaching, but also changing all existing societies into an Islamic society governed by the laws of Allah, known as the Shari'a.

Therefore Islam grants radical Muslims a mandate to change the existing society into an Islamic society, to make Islam supreme, and thus dominate every aspect of society. This is not only the desire of fundamentalists like Osama Bin Laden, but would seem to be the desire of a large number of Muslims all over the world.

This desire is reflected in a document written in 1980 entitled *The Islamic Movement in the West* by Khurram Murad who was then the head of the Islamic Foundation with branches around the world. He outlined his Islamic revolution and the blueprint of how to bring it about in the West.

On page 3 of his document he posed the question: 'What is an Islamic movement?' He goes on to answer: 'An Islamic movement is an organised struggle to change the existing society into an Islamic society based on the Koran and the Sunna, and make Islam, which is a code for entire life, supreme and dominant.'

According to Omar Ahmed, Chairman of the Board of CAIR (Council of American Islamic Relations):

Islam isn't in America to be equal to any other faith, but to become dominant. The Koran should be the highest authority in America, and Islam the only accepted religion on earth.[2]

Such views can find ample justification in the Koran which teaches that Muslims must be supreme over non-Muslims and should be engaged in a jihad to achieve this until the Day of Judgement.

So lose no heart, nor fall into despair. For you must gain mastery, if you are true in faith. Fight those who believe not in Allah nor the Last Day, nor hold that forbidden which hath been forbidden by Allah and His Messenger, nor acknowledge the religion of Truth, (even if they are) of the People of the Book [i.e. Jews and Christians], until they pay the *jizya* [poll tax to be paid by non-Muslims living in a Muslim society] with willing submission, and feel themselves subdued.[3]

This passage from the Koran is a call to Muslims to fight all non-Muslims who do not follow Muhammad's religion. While pagans are to be forcibly converted to Islam, 'the people of the book' (meaning Jews and Christians) are to be fought until they are conquered and then forced to pay the subjugation poll tax, *jizya*. They should then accept the laws of the *dhimmi* ('protected people under Islam' – in effect second-class citizens subservient to the Muslims).

Jihad is more than seeking to persuade others to accept the beliefs of Islam. The Koran teaches that Jihad includes military power:

And make ready against them all you can of power, including steeds of war to threaten the enemy of Allah and your enemy, and others besides whom, you may not know but whom Allah does know. And whatever you shall spend in the Cause of Allah shall be repaid unto you, and you shall not be treated unjustly.[4]

The Western world cannot escape this challenge because its entire industry and infrastructure relies on oil, the commodity which is to be found in super abundance in the lands which are the heart of Islam. At the same time the House of Saud relies on American and Western expertise to run its oil industry, the key to their wealth, and on American forces to defend their land. And while the Western world seeks to extend democratic government worldwide, Saudi Arabia remains one of the most repressive states on earth, with no freedom of expression and association, discrimination against women, no freedom for non-Muslims to practise their faith. Its justice system inflicts harsh use of capital and corporal punishment with frequent public executions and the accused being given very little right to defend themselves before being given long prison sentences often with thousands of lashes inflicted and limbs amputated.

But because Saudi Arabia is so crucial to keeping the world's industrial system going, leaders of Western countries are reluctant to be critical of this. So Saudi Arabia is able to export Islamic fundamentalism throughout the world, which in turn stirs up the hostility towards the West and towards Jews and Christians worldwide.

It all adds up to the House on the Sand relying on the House of Saud.

Notes

1. *Incitement to Jihad on Saudi Government-Controlled TV* by Steven Stalinsky of MEMRI, 24/6/04.
2. Report in the *San Ramon Valley Herald* of a speech to California Muslims in July 1998; quoted by Daniel Pipes in *CAIR: Moderate Friends of Terror*, *New York Post*, April 22, 2002.
3. Sura At-Tawba 9:29 (Koran translation by Yusuf Ali).
4. Sura Al-Anfal 8:60 (Koran translation by Al-Hilali & Khan).

Babylon and Oil

There are two cities which dominate the narrative of the Bible and come to represent the spiritual conflict which is taking place in our world – Babylon and Jerusalem. Incredibly, Babylon and Jerusalem have once again become the focus of the world as we head into the end-time scenario prophesied in the Bible.

On their march to Baghdad during the Gulf War, US forces passed by the site of ancient Babylon, one time capital of a great empire which had its seat of power in the Tigris–Euphrates valley down to the Persian Gulf region. Today the vast deposits of oil in Saudi Arabia, Kuwait, Iraq and Iran are in the area of ancient Babylon.

In the Bible, 'Babylon' has a significance going way beyond the physical region of the city that once dominated the Tigris–Euphrates region in the area now known as Iraq. Its founder, Nimrod (Genesis 10:8–10), was renowned as *'the mighty hunter before the Lord'*. His name in Hebrew may be connected to the verb *marad* – 'to rebel'. In his days an idolatrous religious system was set up, the source of all false religion in the world. In Genesis 11 we read how Babylon was the site of the first attempt at a unified political, economic and religious system in defiance of God, when the Tower of Babel was built in the land of Shinar (another name for the region of Babylon). 'Babel', meaning 'confusion', is the word for 'Babylon' in Hebrew. There God scattered the nations and confused their speech.

In Isaiah 14:12–14 it is revealed that the spiritual power behind Babylon is that of Lucifer (Satan), whose pride and desire to take the place of God caused his downfall:

> *'How are you fallen from heaven,*
> *O Lucifer, son of the morning!*
> *How you are cut down to the ground,*
> *You who weakened the nations!*
> *For you have said in your heart:*
> *"I will ascend into heaven,*
> *I will exalt my throne above the stars of God;*
> *I will also sit on the mount of congregation*
> *On the farthest sides of the north;*
> *I will ascend above the heights of the clouds,*
> *I will be like the Most High." '*

The Hebrew prophets also saw events taking place in the region of Babylon which had to do with the end of days. In Isaiah 13 there is a prophecy about Babylon which deals primarily with events which were to come to pass with the fall of Babylon to the Medes in about 538 BC. This prophecy also has an end-time application with reference to the 'Day of the Lord' when the stars, sun and moon will not give their light and the Lord will punish the world for its evil (verses 10–11). These are all features in both Old and New Testament prophecy for the events surrounding the end of days. In this prophecy it speaks of an army being gathered for battle *'from a far country'* (the Medes were next door to Babylon, so this implies a different event from the fall of Babylon in 538 BC). In the book of Jeremiah we also read that *'a great nation and many kings shall be raised up from the ends of the earth'* to do battle against Babylon (Jeremiah 50:41–42).

The armies of the alliance led by America have moved into the region of ancient Babylon through the two Gulf Wars and the American troops stationed in Saudi Arabia. As we have seen, the oil fields of the region are a vital resource for the whole world and the great powers are desperate to prevent them being taken over by hostile forces which would then threaten their security and prosperity.

It is interesting that the Book of Zechariah (written after the return of the Jewish people from captivity in Babylon, so not about the fall of Babylon in 538 BC) sees a Woman sitting inside a basket with a lead cover over its mouth. The basket is said to represent 'Wickedness' and is carried to Babylon *'to build a house for it in the land of Shinar* [i.e. Babylon]' (Zechariah 5:11). A wicked house coming out of the region of Babylon corrupts the whole earth. Could this have something to do with the oil industry dominated by the countries of the ancient kingdom of Babylon?

If so, it ties up directly with the New Testament prophecy of Revelation 18. Here Babylon becomes the title of a global trading system based on pride and defiance of God infecting all nations with *'the wine of the wrath of her fornication'* (Revelation 18:3–4). This system comes to sudden destruction being burned with fire:

> *In the measure that she glorified herself and lived luxuriously, in the same measure give her torment and sorrow; for she says in her heart, 'I sit as queen, and am no widow, and will not see sorrow.' Therefore her plagues will come in one day – death and mourning and famine. And she will be utterly burned with fire, for strong is the Lord God who judges her. The kings of the earth who committed fornication and lived luxuriously with her will weep and lament for her, when they see the smoke of her burning, standing at a distance for fear of her torment, saying, 'Alas, alas, that great city Babylon, that mighty city! For in one hour your judgment has come.' And the merchants of the earth will weep and mourn over her, for no one buys their merchandise any more.'*

> (Revelation 18:7–11)

Today the region of ancient Babylon is the main source of oil, the commodity on which the entire world trading system relies. After the first Gulf War, the retreating Iraqi troops set fire to the Kuwaiti oil fields, sending plumes of thick black smoke into the atmosphere. A greater environmental catastrophe was only prevented by the prompt action of the engineers who put the fires out. Imagine the scene if the Saudi and Kuwaiti oil fields went up in smoke and there was no one to put the fires out. What would then happen to the world trading system and all the wonderful goods which modern technology has created? It would collapse and no one would buy and sell the merchandise any more.

Ancient Babylon today is the region dominated by the religion of Islam which in its militant form hates the capitalist system of the West and seeks its destruction. It is no accident that the current 'War on Terror' began with Islamic terrorists mainly of Saudi origin destroying the twin towers of the World Trade Center in New York on September 11th, 2001. This was actually a prophetic sign of the much greater destruction which is to come.

Such is the hatred that is driving the Islamist campaign against the West that it does not matter so much to them if their campaign harms their own people as long as it brings down America and the West. Such is the fear of Islam in the West that more and more of our freedoms are being sacrificed in order not to offend the Muslims living in our midst. Despite its cruelty to minorities in its midst, particularly Christians living as second-class citizens or being openly persecuted or even totally suppressed in Islamic countries, politicians, church leaders and the media in the West defer continually to Islamic clerics and in many ways place themselves in a position of submission to Islamic demands.

It is interesting to note that TV news reports now regularly refer to Muhammad as 'The Prophet Muhammad' not just Muhammad. This is clearly in order not to offend Muslim sensitivities. However, they would not refer to the Lord Jesus Christ when talking about Jesus. As a believing Christian I would not expect them to either because calling Jesus 'Lord' is something only a true believer can do. It is an act of faith which comes as a result of receiving Him as Saviour and Lord by the Holy Spirit (1 Corinthians 12:3). Equally, calling Muhammad 'The Prophet' is an act of faith and submission to Allah whereby a person accepts the Islamic claim that Muhammad is the last of the prophets. However, Muhammad's revelation conflicts with the Bible and the Bible makes it clear that God's final word concerning His nature and the way of salvation has been revealed through the Lord Jesus and His apostles. Therefore no believing Christian can call Muhammad 'The Prophet'. Just using this formula in news bulletins in Great Britain is a sign of submission to Islam and rejection of Christianity.

A Canon from Blackburn Cathedral wrote a letter in the local press urging Christians to read a portion of the Koran every day during Ramadan. Can one imagine an imam giving a similar call for Muslims to read the Bible? While the English cricket team was playing the second test in November 2005 in Faisalabad, Pakistan, Christians living in nearby Songua Hill had their churches, homes and amenities burned down by Muslim mobs making false claims that a Koran had been desecrated. There was no mention of this in the BBC news, but imagine if it had been the other way round and Muslims had been attacked.

Some Muslims in France have called for their areas to be treated as a separate entity from the rest of France. The director of the Great Mosque of Paris, Dalil Boubaker, previously suggested that France should be regarded as a 'house of the covenant' by which he appears to mean that France should enter into an agreement with the Muslims to grant them autonomy within the state. French Jewish writer, Bat Ye'or, reveals in her book *Eurabia* that the Arab League and EU governments entered into an agreement some thirty years ago guaranteeing that Muslim immigrants into Europe would not be compelled to adapt in any way 'to the customs of the host countries'.

The British government was defeated on its version of the 'Racial and Religious Hatred Bill' by one vote on January 31st, 2006. This was seen as an answer to prayer by evangelical Christians who opposed it. The government's original bill had been rejected by the House of Lords who carried a watered down version of it which made it a criminal offence to use 'threatening words or behaviour' towards members of a religious group. The government wanted to include the word 'insulting' and this was the issue which caused concern for Christians. The word 'insulting' is open to interpretation. I may consider it legitimate to criticise Islam or to reject Muhammad's claim to be a prophet. However, this may be considered an insult by a Muslim. If he decided to bring action against me because of this it would restrict our freedom to debate differences between religions and in particular make statements critical of Islam. Books like this could be banned. Speaking on BBC Radio's *The Moral Maze* on July 14, 2004 Sir Iqbal Sacranie, Secretary General of the Muslim Council of Britain stated that any 'defamation of the character of the prophet Muhammad would be a direct insult and abuse on the Muslim community'. He indicated that this should be made illegal under the new law.

Already we are seeing that the Muslim religion enjoys immunity from criticism that Christianity has lost and Judaism never had. In the post-Christian West it is much safer to criticize Christian values than Muslim values. Two Christian pastors, Danny Nalliah and Daniel Scot have been on trial in Australia after raising human rights concerns about Islam on a website and at a seminar. They are accused of vilifying Islam and stirring up hatred against Muslims despite the fact that both repeatedly emphasised that Christians should show nothing but love to Muslims.

There is no doubt that the growing power of Islam within the Western world is a result of the dependence of the Western world on oil from the Persian Gulf area, ancient Babylon. This has provided the Islamic world with vast wealth to use in the spreading of Islam and building of mosques throughout the world. It has also made Western governments and media reluctant to criticise Islam and Islamic countries for fear of offending the people who control the oil supply.

Jerusalem the Burdensome Stone

So far we have looked at the influence of oil and Islam on the world scene today and noted they both focus world attention on the region of the Middle East. But there is a third factor which is crucial to our understanding of what is happening both in the Middle East and worldwide. It is the existence of the state of Israel in the region of the Middle East believed by Muslims to be the Dar al Islam (House of Islam – the region in which Muslims are dominant). The existence of this state is a thorn in the flesh to the Islamic world, especially in the light of the victories that Israel has won against Arab Muslim armies and the fact that Israel now controls the city of Jerusalem.

It all adds up to an explosive mix. The Western world needs oil to keep its economy going. Middle Eastern Muslim nations are the main source of oil in the world today. Most of the Islamic world wants to see the end of Israel, and Jerusalem in particular returned to Islamic control as it was from 638 to 1917. Since nations tend to look after their own interests, this means that most nations on earth are willing to sacrifice Israel's interests in order to keep good relations with the Arab Muslim world. They will also be trying to prevent war breaking out because the last time there was a major war between Israel and the Arab world, the Yom Kippur War of 1973, it was followed by the Arab oil boycott and economic recession worldwide.

All of this ties in exactly with the present situation in the Middle East. The Hebrew prophet Zechariah, writing about 2,500 years ago, saw a time coming when Jerusalem will be a *'burdensome stone for all people'* (Zechariah 12:3, AV). In other words, the issue of who rules Jerusalem, the heart of the Arab Israeli conflict, will involve all the nations of the world. I often think of Zechariah writing these words down and wonder if he thought, 'That's a bit over the top, Lord. Surely you don't mean all nations, you just mean those nations around Israel, like Lebanon, Syria, Jordan, Egypt, Arabia.' Imagine Zechariah turning up in England or America or China in his own day and being able to communicate with the people there and telling them that what was happening in Jerusalem was vital to their interests. They would not have known where it was and even if he told them all about what was happening there it would not have made a scrap of difference to their lives.

Fortunately Zechariah was not a modern theologian so he did not scrub out the bits he did not understand. Today we see a situation whereby all the nations are involved in what happens in Jerusalem. Modern technology means we can see and hear about events taking place there the moment they are happening. Jerusalem has more foreign journalists per head of population than any other place on earth. The interests of Jews, Christians and Muslims worldwide mean that about half the population of the world have some interest in the situation in this relatively small city perched on the top of the Judean hills. The organisation representing all nations, the United Nations, has passed more resolutions over the situation in Jerusalem than any other comparable situation anywhere in the world. Peace plans like the Oslo Accords and the Road Map are constantly being put forward, modified and also failing to deliver.

When Israel withdrew its settlements from Gaza in August 2005 many in Israel hoped that they would be able to make a peace deal with the Palestinians which would still give them control over parts of the West Bank and Jerusalem. However, as far as the Palestinians and most of the world are concerned this withdrawal was only the beginning of a process whose minimum demand is the return of all the territories occupied by Israel since 1967. Palestinian President, Mahmoud Abbas said on August 13th, 2005, 'The Palestinians are celebrating today liberating Gaza Strip, and will tomorrow, by God willing, celebrate the liberation of Jerusalem. Here is the spring-board from which our public will start to build the Palestinian state with Jerusalem as its capital.' He added further, that the motto of the campaign is 'Today Gaza and Tomorrow the West Bank and Jerusalem'. Israelis were infuriated to find that the UN Development Programme has funded the making of thousands of banners, bumper stickers, mugs, and T-shirts bearing this slogan being widely distributed to Palestinians in the Gaza Strip.

The shock election victory of Hamas over the Fateh party in the Palestinian elections in January 2006 means that the government of the Palestinian Authority is now in the hands of people who are committed to the elimination of Israel. The Charter of the Hamas movement makes this absolutely clear:

Article Six
The Islamic Resistance Movement [Hamas] is a distinct Palestinian Movement which owes its loyalty to Allah, derives from Islam its way of life and strives to raise the banner of Allah over every inch of Palestine [i.e. Israel and the West Bank and Gaza must ultimately become one Arab Muslim entity].

Article Eight
Allah is its goal, the Prophet its model, the Qur'an its Constitution, Jihad its path and death for the case of Allah its most sublime belief [i.e. this is as unchangeable as the Qur'an is for the Muslim].

Article Eleven
The Islamic Resistance Movement believes that the land of Palestine has been an Islamic Waqf [a possession of Muslims which cannot be given to non-Muslims] throughout the generations and until the Day of Resurrection, no one can renounce it or part of it, or abandon it or part of it ... This is the status [of the land] in Islamic Shari'a, and it is similar to all lands conquered by Islam by force, and made thereby Waqf lands upon their conquest, for all generations of Muslims until the Day of Resurrection [i.e. any land

once Islamic must be returned to Islamic rule and remain so until the end of the world. No treaty or agreement which contradicts this has any validity].

Before the election, Hamas leader Khaled Mash'al spoke at a rally in Damascus broadcast on Al-Jazeera TV (30/12/05):

'Who can tell, my brothers and sisters, when we will celebrate, on this podium, the liberation of the West Bank? When will we celebrate the liberation of Jaffa, Haifa, Safed, and the Negev? When will we celebrate the departure of the last Zionist from our land? Yes. Some people ask when this will happen. Say: It could be soon. Such is our faith in Allah. We have no doubt that victory will come, and that just as we liberated Palestine from the Crusaders and from the Mongols, we will regain it – pure and purified – from the Zionist occupiers.'

After the election he stated on Al-Jazeera TV (31/1/06) that the election to power would not change this charter by one word:

'We are committed to the resistance and adhere to its weapons . . . As for recognizing [Israel] and amending our charter, Hamas is not the kind of movement that succumbs to pressure . . . We will not recognize it, no matter how much time passes . . . We believe in acting according to stages . . . '

The reference to stages shows Hamas is following the original plan agreed to by the PLO in 1974. Known as the '10 Points Phased Doctrine' this strategy aimed to set up a mini-state as the first step in 'liberating Palestine'. The statement of the Palestine National Council said, amongst other things:

Once it is established, the Palestinian national authority will strive to achieve a union of the confrontation countries, with the aim of completing the liberation of all Palestinian territory and as a step along the road to comprehensive Arab unity.

In other words, this state would be a springboard for the final goal, which is the elimination of Israel.

Although this is the ultimate goal, Hamas has said that it will consider the possibility of a long-term truce, not a lasting peace with Israel, as long as Israel withdraws from all the lands occupied in 1967. Fascinatingly the figure of somewhere between five years and ten years has been put forward. The prophecy of Daniel 9:27 is interpreted by many to speak of a seven-year peace treaty which will be made with Israel in the last days and which will break down half-way through.

Any talk of peace is of course deceptive and Hamas and the Islamic radicals view victory over Israel as the first stage in their goal of world conquest for Islam. This was made very clear by a speech given by Khaled Mash'al in Damascus and broadcast on al-Jazeera TV on February 3rd, 2006:

> We say to this West by Allah, you will be defeated. We apologize to our Prophet Muhammad, but we say to him: Oh Prophet of Allah, do not be saddened, your nation will be victorious. We say to this West, which does not act reasonably, and does not learn its lessons: By Allah, you will be defeated. You will be defeated in Palestine, and your defeat there has already begun. True, it is Israel that is being defeated there, but when Israel is defeated, its path is defeated, those who call to support it are defeated, and the cowards who hide behind it and support it are defeated. Israel will be defeated, and so will whoever supported or supports it.
>
> America will be defeated in Iraq. Wherever the Islamic nation is targeted, its enemies will be defeated, Allah willing. The nation of Muhammad is gaining victory in Palestine. The nation of Muhammad is gaining victory in Iraq, and it will be victorious in all Arab and Muslim lands. 'Their multitudes will be defeated and turn their backs and flee.' These fools will be defeated, the wheel of time will turn, and times of victory and glory will be upon our nation, and the West will be full of remorse, when it is too late.
>
> They think that history has ended with them. They do not know that the law of Allah cannot be changed or replaced. 'You

shall not find a substitute for the law of Allah. You shall not find any change to the law of Allah.' Today, the Arab and Islamic nation is rising and awakening, and it will reach its peak, Allah willing. It will be victorious. It will link the present to the past. It will open up the horizons of the future. It will regain the leadership of the world. Allah willing, the day is not far off.

I say to the European countries: Hurry up and apologize to our nation, because if you do not, you will regret it. This is because our nation is progressing and is victorious. Do not leave a black mark in the collective memory of the nation, because our nation will not forgive you. *Tomorrow, our nation will sit on the throne of the world. This is not a figment of the imagination, but a fact. Tomorrow we will lead the world, Allah willing.* Apologize today, before remorse will do you no good. Our nation is moving forwards, and it is in your interest to respect a victorious nation.

Our nation will be victorious. When it reaches the leadership of the world, and controls its own decisions, then it will prevent this overt interference in our affairs, and its pillaging of natural resources, and will prevent these recurring offences against our land, against our nation, and against our holy places – then you will regret it.

Before Israel dies, it must be humiliated and degraded. Allah willing, before they die, they will experience humiliation and degradation every day. America will be of no avail to them. Their generals will be of no avail to them. The last of their generals has been forgotten. Allah has made him disappear. He's over. Gone is that Sharon behind whose back they would hide and find shelter, and with whom they would feel relatively secure. Today they have frail leaders, who don't even know where our Lord placed them. Allah willing, we will make them lose their eyesight, we will make them lose their brains.

Their weapons will be of no avail to them. Their nuclear weapons will be of no use to them. They thought that they had hegemony over the region with their nuclear weapons, but suddenly Pakistan popped up with Islamic nuclear weapons, and they are afraid of Iran and several Arab countries have some chemical weapons.

Israel has begun to sense that its superiority has come to an end. Its army, which has superior conventional weapons – the air force, the armoured corps, and the missiles – there are no longer wars in which these are used.

As a manifesto for Armageddon you cannot get much clearer than this. However, most of the media and the politicians in the West choose to turn a blind eye to this hate filled religious fanaticism which aims to subjugate the whole world and sees the defeat of Israel as the first stage in this process. News reports and political commentaries generally present the view that hostility to Israel is caused by the fact that Israel occupied Arab territories in 1967. The reality is that hostility to Israelis is caused by the fact that Israel exists. If Israel gives in to every demand of Hamas and hands over all the land occupied in 1967 including Jerusalem they will not receive peace in exchange.

There is nothing new in this. Before 1967 the Arab world aimed to eliminate the state of Israel, as Nasser of Egypt made clear in the build up to the Six Day War when he said, on May 27th, 1967, 'Our basic objective will be the destruction of Israel.' The PLO was formed in 1964 not to liberate the West Bank and Gaza from Israeli control as they were then ruled by Jordan and Egypt respectively. It was formed to eliminate Israel and replace it with a Palestinian state from the River Jordan to the Mediterranean.

The Fateh party which Hamas has replaced was derived from the PLO. Despite 'peace' initiatives signed by Yasser Arafat, and agreed to by other leaders of the Fateh party, there is plenty of evidence that the destruction of Israel remained their aim also. Palestinian children have been systematically indoctrinated to hate Israelis in their schools, in their mosques, on their TV programmes. We have a video showing clips of children as young as three years old being taught to hate and kill Jews.

Throughout the Arab and Muslim world there has been a flood of incitement not just against Israel, but also against all Jewish people. Mahathir Mohammad, the long-serving Prime Minister of Malaysia who stepped down on October 31st 2003, after twenty-two years in power, used his speech at the opening session of the fifty-seven-state Organisation of the Islamic Conference (OIC) in Putrajaya, Malaysia, on October 16th 2003, to argue that the Jews control the world: 'They invented socialism, communism, human rights and democracy so that persecuting them would appear to be wrong; so that they can enjoy equal rights with others. With these they have gained control of the most powerful countries and they, this tiny community, have become a world power.' He also said that, 'The Europeans killed six million Jews out of twelve million, but today the Jews rule the world by proxy. They get others to fight and die for them.' The speech got a standing ovation from the assembled kings, presidents, sheikhs and emirs.

The idea of a Jewish conspiracy ruling the world was first put out in *The Protocols of the Elders of Zion*, which was circulated in Tsarist Russia to foment anti-Semitism and used by Hitler as one of the foundations of his programme to exterminate the Jewish people. Today the same myth is being propagated in the Muslim world to demonise the Jews as part of the campaign against the existence of Israel. The *Protocols* have been translated into Arabic and widely circulated in the Arab world. Egyptian TV broadcast a forty-part adaptation of the *Protocols* called 'Horsemen without a Horse'.

Writing in *The Guardian* (14/12/03) William Shawcross reported on the new face of anti-Semitism in the Arab world:

> In Berlin last weekend I saw clips from hideous films that portrayed Jews as (literally) bloodsucking murderers. In one episode 'rabbis' sliced up a Jew and poured boiling lead into his mouth because he had slept with a non-Jewish woman. In another, rabbis murdered a Christian child to use his blood to bake Passover matzos. The dialogue in the latter went like this:
>
> Rabbi: 'Well, we have a mission from the leadership, and we must carry it out quickly.'
>
> Young Jewish Man: 'What is it?'

Rabbi: 'Listen. We want the blood of a Christian child before Passover, for the matzos.'

The film then shows the terrified child, Joseph, being brought in to have his throat cut over a metal bowl. In the next scene the rabbi insists that another Jewish man eat some matzos.

Rabbi: 'You must eat this, if not for my sake, for the sake of God.'

Jewish man: 'Thank you.'

Rabbi: 'How is it? Tasty?'

Jewish man: 'Plain. Like all the matzos in the world.'

Rabbi: 'No. Make no mistake. This one is tastier and holier because it was kneaded with pure blood, the blood of Joseph.'

These films were horrifying and impossible to watch. But the worst thing was that they were not relics of Nazi propaganda, borrowed from a dusty Berlin archive. I wish. No, these films were made recently in Syria, with the help of the Syrian government and were broadcast in twenty-nine episodes last month by a Lebanese television station, Al-Manar, during Ramadan. According to a report on 11 November by the *Syria Times*, they are part of 'a Syrian TV series recording the criminal history of Zionism'.

This hatred is reinforced by sermons from mosques encouraging terrorism against Israel. The following is an extract from a sermon given by Imam Sheikh Ibrahim Madhi in Gaza on April 12th, 2002 and broadcast live on Palestinian TV. It is typical of the kind of incitement being given today in mosques throughout the Islamic world.

We are convinced of the future victory of Allah; we believe that one of these days, we will enter Jerusalem as conquerors, enter Jaffa as conquerors, enter Haifa as conquerors, and all of Palestine as conquerors, as Allah has decreed. [By referring to Haifa and Jaffa, Israeli coastal cities, he means that the Muslims will eliminate Israel.] Anyone who does not attain martyrdom in these days should wake in the middle of the night and say: 'My

God, why have you deprived me of martyrdom for your sake? For the martyr lives next to Allah.'

The Jews await the false Jewish messiah, while we await, with Allah's help the Mahdi and Jesus, peace be upon him. Jesus' pure hands will murder the false Jewish messiah. Where? In the city of Lod, in Palestine. Palestine will be, as it was in the past, a graveyard for the invaders. A reliable *hadith* [tradition] says: 'The Jews will fight you, but you will be set to rule over them.' What could be more beautiful than this tradition? 'The Jews will fight you' – that is, the Jews have begun to fight us. 'You will be set to rule over them' – Who will set the Muslim to rule over the Jew? Allah. When the Jew hides behind the rock and the tree, the rock and tree will say: 'Oh Muslim, oh servant of Allah, a Jew hides behind me, come and kill him.'

In explanation of the reference to Jesus in this quotation, Muslims believe Jesus is a prophet, but not divine. The Koran contains stories about Jesus which change the events to fit in with this view. Muslims also have a number of beliefs about the second coming of Jesus based on the *hadith* (traditions) rather than the Koran. They believe he will come back as 'a man of medium height, reddish hair, wearing two light yellow garments' (*Sunan Abu-Dawud*, Book 37, Number 4310); that he will land on the minaret of the mosque in Damascus when he will invite the whole world, including Jews and Christians, to become Muslims (*Hadith* 814). He will then destroy the Daijal (a kind of Antichrist figure in Islamic thinking) at Lydda (Lod) in Israel, slaughter the Jews and cause the Christian religion to become extinct. He will then live for forty years, marry and have children and perform the Hajj (pilgrimage) to Mecca. Then he will die and be buried beside the grave of Muhammad. Thus Islam gives a view of the events described in the Bible for the end of days which is almost the exact opposite in the direction it takes.

Hatred for Israel and blaming Israel for all that is going wrong in the world is now becoming standard fare not just in the Middle East but in Europe and much of the Christian Church as well. The call by the Presbyterian Church of the USA for a boycott of Israel as an apartheid state has now been followed by a similar call from a delegation from the Anglican Church. A delegation of the 'Anglican Peace and Justice Network' visiting Israel and the Palestinian territories in September 2004 calls for 'for divestment from Israel . . . so that Christian faiths can bring peace to this land'.

The only kind of peace that this kind of church is helping to bring about is one caused by the destruction of Israel. The Church singles out Israel for economic boycott, while ignoring the persecution of Christians in Muslim lands, including the areas controlled by the Palestinian Authority where traditionally Christian towns like Bethlehem are becoming dominated by Islam as Christians leave their homes because of Islamic intolerance and persecution.

A report in the newspaper of Iraqi émigrés living in London (14/11/04) states:

> Approximately 4 million Lebanese Christians have emigrated from their country as a result of the pressures placed upon them by others. About half a million Iraqi Christians have left their country for the same reasons . . . The situation gets worse today because of the discrimination by Islamic fundamentalist extremists. In Palestine, the Christians are becoming almost extinct as a result of the control of extremist Muslims on the Palestinian issue and the marginalisation of the role of the Christians, apart from the negative impact of the Intifada, which is led by Islamist organisations, on the Christians of Palestine. With regard to Christians in Egypt, the Copts, what happened and is happening to them equally on the part of the state and the Islamists will suffice to fill pages of books and newspapers to explain the coercion, discrimination and persecution. What is happening in Algeria, Mauritania, Somalia, and others is too long to explain.

> This situation is also reflected in non-Arab Muslim countries. In Islamic countries like Pakistan, Indonesia and Nigeria, Christians suffer from persecution. In Pakistan, Islamist spiritual leaders have issued a fatwa [religious decree] permitting the

killing of two Christians for every Muslim killed by the American attacks in Afghanistan, as though the Americans represent Christianity in the world. In other countries the Christians live in fear, under the shadow of threat, and face a growing cycle of assaults whenever the United States and its allies carry out a military operation against any country.

Christians are afraid of what might happen to them in these countries. The situation is quite critical and requires urgent attention. It is difficult for us to imagine any other time in which the Christians have felt a greater danger than the danger they feel today in these countries.

You would think this situation would be the main concern of the churches in the West, not attacking tiny Israel, fighting for its life against Islamic inspired hatred. Israel is the only country in the Middle East where Arab Christians have freedom to express their opinions and organise their communities without state interference. Yet it is the only country in the Middle East which many leading representatives of various denominations of the church target for condemnation and ultimately for destruction.

As if this were not bad enough, the UN has passed more resolutions condemning Israel than any other situation in the world. On July 20th, 2004, the UN General Assembly passed a resolution condemning Israel's security barrier and demanding that it comply with the ruling of the International Court of Justice (ICJ) at The Hague. The ICJ ruled that the buffer is illegal and must be removed and that compensation should be paid to the Palestinians it affects. The United States, Micronesia, the Marshall Islands, Palau and Australia sided with Israel and voted 'No' while the entire European Union (including Britain) voted in favour of the measure. Israel's UN Ambassador Dan Gillerman reacted angrily saying, 'It is simply outrageous to respond with such vigour to a measure that saves lives and respond with such casual indifference and apathy to the ongoing campaign of Palestinian terrorism that takes lives. This is not justice but a perversion of justice.'

The United Nations held a 'Day of Solidarity with the Palestinian People' in December 2005. A large map of 'Palestine', with Israel literally wiped off the map, featured prominently in the festivities. The ceremony was held at the UN headquarters in New York and was attended by Secretary General Kofi Annan and the Presidents of the UN Security Council and the General Assembly.

During the festivities, a map labelled a 'map of Palestine' was displayed prominently between UN and PLO flags. The map, with 'Palestine' written in Arabic atop it, did not include Israel, a member of the UN for fifty-six years. With the map hanging behind him, Secretary-General Annan addressed the public meeting at UN Headquarters.

At the start of the ceremony, the dignitaries present asked attendees to observe a moment of silence. 'I invite everyone present to rise and observe a minute of silence in memory of all those who have given their lives for the cause of the Palestinian people,' the master of ceremonies said, 'and the return of peace between Israel and Palestine.'

At the same time as condemning Israel, the UN takes only very feeble measures against Sudan where systematic abuses of human rights have been going on for the past fifteen years. The Sudanese government came to power in 1989 and declared an Islamic state, imposing Arabic culture and Islamic Shari'a law on the people of Southern Sudan in an attempt to destroy their African culture. Africans from the south, including many Christians, were crushed, with the government perpetrating murder, torture, slavery and forced conversions to Islam while the UN and the world did nothing. Now the people of the Darfur region of Sudan have received the same treatment although the vast majority are Muslims.

Commenting on this Melanie Phillips writes:

> How can the UN be the world's policeman when it dignifies tyrants and mass murderers and cynically seats them in moral judgement over the rest of the world? The brutal truth is that the UN not only refuses to confront tyranny and terror, but actually defends it and provides it with a global platform. It has never

passed a single resolution condemning China, Syria or Saudi Arabia, despite those countries' abuse of human rights, absence of democracy or sponsorship of terror. Last year it defeated a resolution criticising Zimbabwe, a nation left hungry and oppressed by a brutal tyrant. Yet at the same time it demands that Israel destroy the security barrier it has erected to defend its citizens from Palestinian terror ... The UN cannot fight tyranny and terror because it is itself an organisation riddled with corruption which appeases, connives at and even promotes tyranny and terror ... The UN stands at the apex of a moral world order which is broken and bankrupt. It is a tyrants' club and Sudan is its latest tragic casualty.

(*Daily Mail*, 23/7/04)

However, it is clear that Israel will not just lie down and accept the death sentence being passed on it by the majority of nations in the modern world. Jewish people know they have only one state in the world and that if this one goes there will be no other place on earth where they can set up an alternative Jewish homeland. Because of their unique history of persecution and the strength of their armed forces the state of Israel can be expected to defend itself against those who come to kill and maim its citizens no matter what the world may say against them.

The condemnation of Israel and the blind eye being turned to the systematic abuse of human rights in the Arab and Muslim world is not only a source of shame on the modern world. It is also a fulfilment of prophecy which sees the nations of the world coming against Israel in the last days of this age. The spiritual reason why Jerusalem and the land of Israel is such a focus of world attention is the fact that this is the place that God has chosen by the covenant made with Abraham which gave the title deeds of ownership of the land to Abraham's descendants through Isaac and Jacob. The nations coming against Israel are fulfilling the words of Psalm 83:4:

'Come, and let us cut them off from being a nation,
That the name of Israel may be remembered no more.'

In verses 6–8 of this psalm there is a list of nations, which can be identified with Jordan, Egypt, Lebanon, Gaza, Syria and Iraq. In 1948, 1967 and 1973 Israel has had to fight wars for survival against superior armies from these countries bent on pushing the Jewish state into the sea.

In this psalm there is a reference to Zebah and Zalmunna, '*Who said, "Let us take for ourselves the pastures of God for a possession"* ' (verse 12). We find reference to Zebah and Zalmunna in Judges 8. They were kings of Midian, leaders of the army, which came against Israel in the days of Gideon. In Judges 8:21 we read: '*Gideon arose and killed Zebah and Zalmunna, and took the crescent ornaments that were on their camels' necks*'. The Hebrew word used for 'ornaments' is *ha saharonim*, an unusual word, which is correctly translated in the New King James Version as 'crescent ornaments'. The crescent ornament showed dedication to the moon god of paganism.

Today there is a world religion, which also uses the crescent as its symbol – Islam. Islam embodies everything spoken of in this psalm in its attitude towards Israel. It is the dominant religion of the countries, which surround Israel. Those countries have made an alliance against Israel aiming at the elimination of the Jewish state. While they may work with the UN and the powers of the world today to propose a treaty, which offers 'peace', their real aim is the destruction of Israel.

The Bible is clear that the last war of this age will be fought over Israel and Jerusalem. Armageddon, referred to in Revelation 16:16, is a word that has gone into the popular vocabulary as the great war which will end all wars, but in Hebrew it means the mount of Megiddo, a place in the northern plains of Israel where the armies of the world will gather for the final conflict. As these armies head south for Jerusalem they will meet their doom not as a result of action by the Israeli Defence Force or the US army but as the Lord Himself returns in power and glory:

> Then the LORD will go forth
> And fight against those nations,

As He fights in the day of battle.
And in that day His feet will stand on the Mount of Olives,
Which faces Jerusalem on the east . . .
And the LORD *shall be King over all the earth.*

(Zechariah 14:3–4, 9)

Now I saw heaven opened, and behold, a white horse. And He who sat on him was called Faithful and True, and in righteousness He judges and makes war . . . And the armies in heaven, clothed in fine linen, white and clean, followed Him on white horses. Now out of His mouth goes a sharp sword, that with it He should strike the nations. And He Himself will rule them with a rod of iron. He Himself treads the winepress of the fierceness and wrath of Almighty God. And He has on His robe and on His thigh a name written:

KING OF KINGS AND LORD OF LORDS.

(Revelation 19:11, 14–16)

The result of the Lord Jesus returning in power is the absolute defeat of the allied powers of evil. He will then set up the thousand-year reign of the Messiah on earth, a prelude to the eternal state, in which there really will be peace and safety at last for this planet. The fact that both Jerusalem and Babylon are centre stage in world events today is a major sign that we are living in the days leading up to the end of this age and the return of the Lord Jesus.

Environmental Disasters and the End of the Age

One of the major concerns of people today is environmental destruction. There is a direct link between this and our modern technological society. Past ways of travel, agriculture and building were all renewable and had no impact on the environment. Not so our modern society. More and more people are waking up to the fact that we are fouling up the only planet we can live on and it may be too late to reverse the process.

The evidence of climate change, particularly from areas where it can be measured most clearly, the poles and the deserts, show that our climate is heating up. Of course there are those who deny that there is any connection between the burning of fossil fuels, in particular oil and coal, and global warming. Dr Sami Solanki, director of the Max Planck Institute for Solar System Research in Göttingen, Germany, says dramatic weather changes are caused not by man-made activity, but the result of the sun heating up, which 'may now be affecting global temperatures'. Max Mayfield, head of the National Hurricane Center in Miami, and hurricane forecaster William Gray, a professor of atmospheric science at Colorado State University, say the current 'onslaught of storms is very much natural'.

It is hard to believe what has been occurring recently is simply 'very much natural'. The succession and intensity of these events have rightly caused people to sense something is not right with the earth, and the future is precarious to say the least.

Following the devastation caused by Hurricane Katrina a number of public figures in the USA put the blame for the disaster on global warming. Senator Robert Kennedy wrote in *The Huffington Post* (29/8/05):

> The science is clear. This month, a study published in the journal *Nature* by a renowned MIT climatologist linked the increasing prevalence of destructive hurricanes to human-induced global warming. Now we are all learning what it's like to reap the whirlwind of fossil fuel dependence. Our destructive addiction has given us a catastrophic war in the Middle East and now Katrina is giving our nation a glimpse of the climate chaos we are bequeathing our children.

Ross Gelbspan wrote in *The Boston Globe* (30/8/05):

> The hurricane that struck Louisiana yesterday was nicknamed Katrina by the National Weather Service. Its real name is global warming. When the year began with a two-foot snowfall in Los Angeles, the cause was global warming. When a severe drought in the Midwest dropped water levels in the Missouri River to their lowest on record earlier this summer, the reason was global warming. In July, when the worst drought on record triggered wildfires in Spain and Portugal and left water levels in France at their lowest in thirty years, the explanation was global warming. When a lethal heat wave in Arizona kept temperatures above 110 degrees and killed more than twenty people in one week, the culprit was global warming. And when the Indian city of Bombay (Mumbai) received 37 inches of rain in one day killing 1,000 people and disrupting the lives of 20 million others the villain was global warming.
>
> As the atmosphere warms, it generates longer droughts, more-intense downpours, more-frequent heat waves, and more-severe storms. Although Katrina began as a relatively small hurricane that glanced off south Florida, it was supercharged with extra-ordinary intensity by the relatively blistering sea surface

temperatures in the Gulf of Mexico. The consequences are as heartbreaking as they are terrifying.

Unfortunately, very few people in America know the real name of Hurricane Katrina because the coal and oil industries have spent millions of dollars to keep the public in doubt about the issue. The reason is simple: To allow the climate to stabilize requires humanity to cut its use of coal and oil by 70 percent. That, of course, threatens the survival of one of the largest commercial enterprises in history.

In 1995, public utility hearings in Minnesota found that the coal industry had paid more than $1 million to four scientists who were public dissenters on global warming. And Exxon Mobil has spent more than $13 million since 1998 on an anti-global warming public relations and lobbying campaign. In 2000, big oil and big coal scored their biggest electoral victory yet when President George W. Bush was elected president – and subsequently took suggestions from the industry for his climate and energy policies.

As the pace of climate change accelerates, many researchers fear we have already entered a period of irreversible runaway climate change. Against this background, the ignorance of the American public about global warming stands out as an indictment of the US media.

A record loss of sea ice in the Arctic in the summer of 2005 has convinced scientists that the climate of the northern hemisphere may have reached the point of no return. They believe global warming is melting the Arctic ice so rapidly that the region is beginning to absorb more heat from the sun, causing the ice to melt still further and so reinforcing a vicious cycle of melting and heating. The greatest fear is that the Arctic has reached a point beyond which nothing can reverse the eventual loss of sea ice and with it the massive glaciers of Greenland which will raise sea levels dramatically. If all the land ice on Greenland were to melt it would raise sea levels around the world by six metres, enough to flood the major population centres of nearly every country with a coastline (*The Independent*, 16/9/05).

According to an article in *The Times* (12/7/05) the Himalayas' melting glaciers will open the floodgates to catastrophe. It will begin with overflowing rivers, which will wash away homes and fields in China, India and South-East Asia. After a few decades will come drought, as the same rivers dwindle to a trickle. And then will come the second deluge – immense walls of water, like mountain tsunamis, which will break through thin walls of frozen earth, washing away bridges, dams and Himalayan communities. Countless people will drown or die from the inevitable epidemics and food shortages. Many more will lose their livelihoods and be condemned to poverty in some of the most densely populated areas of the world. And, most alarming of all, it may be too late to do anything about it.

The Himalayan glaciers supply 8.6 million cubic metres every year to Asian rivers, including the Yangtze and Yellow rivers in China, the Ganges in India, the Indus in Pakistan, the Brahmaputra in Bangladesh, the Salween and Irrawaddy in Burma, and the Mekong, which flows through China, Burma, Thailand, Laos, Cambodia and Vietnam. But the average temperature in the Himalayas has risen by 1°C since the 1970s, and the glaciers are in retreat. The Khumbu Glacier in Nepal, where Sir Edmund Hillary and Tenzing Norgay began their ascent of Everest, has retreated more than three miles since they climbed the mountain in 1953. According to a report published in March by the World Wildlife Fund, a quarter of the world's glaciers could disappear by 2050.

At the same time the deserts of the world are advancing. Early every spring, dust blown over from Inner Mongolia descends on the Chinese capital, Beijing. The first Beijing residents notice is an orange glow in the air, then a choking haze descends. Most of the dust in these increasingly frequent storms originates far to the north, on Inner Mongolia's once rolling grassland plains, which are turning into desert. Official figures show more than 770 square miles of China turns to desert every year. The causes are complex – over-grazing and bad agricultural management play a large role – but north China's changing climate is undeniably linked to global warming. Long-term records show a declining rainfall and temperatures have risen at twice the global average.

Four Brazilian cities in the Amazon jungle state of Amazonas were declared disaster areas in the November 2005 as the worst drought in sixty years dried up rivers that thousands of families depend on to receive food and medicine. With the rivers drying up drinking water has also become scarce. The little water that exists in the rivers is polluted. Another seventeen cities and towns declared a state of alert. The Amazon rain forest known as the 'lungs of the world' has been ruthlessly cut down by burning trees in order to increase quick profit from the land. As the trees are cut down the rains cease and the land turns to dust.

A group of British aid agencies and environmental groups, from Oxfam to Greenpeace, produced a report, *Africa – Up In Smoke?*, insisting the issues of African poverty and climate change are inseparably linked, and the first cannot be solved without dealing with the second. It was a direct challenge to the simple Live8 theme, that if only the economic basis of Africa's future can be sorted by a properly responsible rich world, the continent will come good. It will not, the report said, if we do not tackle the warming atmosphere. For everything that makes Africa hard to inhabit today will be made harder by global warming. Hunger will be made more acute; shortage of clean water will be more degrading; disease will be more painful, crippling and deadly; natural disasters will be more overwhelming.

Global warming may not make the weather hotter in all cases. Britain and northern Europe are kept mild in the winter due to the influence of the Gulf Stream which brings warm water and air up from the Caribbean. Without it winter temperatures would plunge to $-20°C$. So the news that the Gulf Stream has begun to weaken abruptly could be one of the most important and most devastating scientific observations of out time. Researchers at the National Oceanographic Centre in Southampton who have measured the strength of the current far out into the Atlantic have found that it has slowed by a massive 30%. Robert Sagosian, director of the Woods Hole Oceanographic Institution in Massachusetts warns:

'We may be approaching a threshold that would shut down the Gulf Stream and cause abrupt climate changes. Large regions may experience a precipitous shift into colder climates.' Paradoxically the scientists are saying that this abrupt cooling could be the result of global warming melting the Arctic ice-caps. This would interfere with the vast natural pumps in the Arctic Ocean that power the Gulf Stream.

In addition to these worldwide events there are direct effects of industrialisation on the environment. All tap water in the Chinese city of Harbin, with a population of 3.5 million, was cut off for several days in November 2005 following an explosion at a petro-chemical plant downstream which released about 100 tons of benzene into the Songhua River. The Chinese government is growing increasingly concerned at the devastating effects of the country's appalling environmental record and its effect on its rivers at a time when water is already in short supply. In June the deputy construction minister said that 90% of cities, all major rivers and three quarters of the country's lakes suffer water pollution.

A report launched at the Royal Society in London and backed by 1,360 scientists from ninety-five countries warns that almost two-thirds of the natural machinery that supports life on Earth is being degraded by human pressure. Irretrievable damage is being done to the wetlands, forests, savannahs, estuaries, coastal fisheries and other habitats that recycle air, water and nutrients for all living creatures. 'Human activity is putting such a strain on the natural functions of Earth that the ability of the planet's eco-systems to sustain future generations can no longer be taken for granted,' it says. 'In many cases, it is literally a matter of living on borrowed time. By using up supplies of fresh groundwater faster than they can be recharged, for example, we are depleting assets at the expense of our children. We may have distanced our-selves from nature, but we rely completely on the services it delivers.'

At the same time there has been a great increase in killer earthquakes. On December 26th, 2003, the Iranian town of Bam was devastated by an earthquake measuring 6.5 on the

Richter scale and killing more than 26,000 people. Exactly one year later on December 26th, 2004, the tsunami disaster devastated coastal regions of Indonesia, Sri Lanka, India and Thailand killing around 200,000 people. The underwater earthquake measured 9 on the Richter scale and caused the earth to wobble slightly on its axis. On October 8th the earthquake in the mountains of Pakistan killed over 50,000 and left hundreds of thousands homeless.

One explanation given to the increase in disasters is the controversial Gaia Theory, named after the earth goddess of the ancient Greeks. This theory was developed by the British scientist James Lovelock during the 1960s while he was working on the Viking project looking into the possibility of life on Mars. As he considered what sustained life on Earth and observed the earth's atmosphere with its delicate balance of oxygen, hydrogen, nitrogen, methane, and traces of other elements, he came up with the idea of the earth as a living and interdependent whole, capable of regulating itself to eliminate injury like a body dealing with illness or injury.

According to this idea the earth is one immense and eternally interacting living system – a living planet, floating in space, every part of its great engine affecting every other, for good or for ill. The Earth has some organs which are especially important, such as the rain forest and wetlands, which are more vital to the global environment than are other parts of the system. Using the comparison of the human body, it is possible to lose a minor part like the big toe and survive, but if you lose a major part like the lungs you are dead. So the Earth may lose some animal species due to human carelessness of the environment and survive, but if a vital organ is threatened then it must fight back against human interference or die.

In some quarters of the environmental movement the idea is being put forward that the disasters coming on the earth are the result of Gaia issuing a wake up call to humanity to stop destroying the only planet we can live on. In other words Gaia may take action to bring a kind of judgment on humanity for fouling up the planet. According to this view then disasters are the earth fighting back against human degradation of the planet. This leads to the New Age view that we need to get back into oneness with the planet and each other to save the earth.

The Bible teaches a different concept – that the personal God who made the earth and gave humanity the task of looking after it is speaking through these events, which He actually foretold through the prophets and the Lord Jesus centuries ago. It is true that the earth is an interdependent whole which was created by God as *'very good'*. Everything required for life is held in delicate balance on the only planet we can live on. The distance of the earth from the sun, the atmosphere, the water cycle, the topsoil for growing food, everything is exactly right for sustaining life. The evolutionary idea that it all came about by a cosmic accident is as absurd as the possibility of the computer I am using to write this book coming into existence as a result of atoms assembling themselves in the right order to make a computer. Design demands a designer and creation demands a creator. There is abundant evidence for those who care to look for it that God as Creator, not random evolution, has the answer to the question of how we came to be here.

According to the Genesis account humanity was to have *'dominion'* over the earth, not in the sense of plundering it, but of caring for the earth and its creatures (Genesis 1:26–28; Psalm 8) in harmony with God our Creator. But human disobedience to God caused the degradation of the earth with first the Fall (Genesis 3) and then the Flood (Genesis 6–8) upsetting the delicate balance of the original creation.

When we go to the other end of the biblical time scale and look at the events of the end of this age it is clear that disasters affecting the earth are going to increase in the last days of this age. Jesus said concerning the days before His second coming,

> *'There will be great earthquakes in various places, and famines and pestilences; and there will be fearful sights and great signs from heaven … And there will be signs in the sun, in the moon and in the stars; and on the earth distress of nations, with perplexity, **the sea and the waves***

roaring; men's hearts failing them from fear and the expectation of those
things which are coming on the earth, for the powers of the heavens
will be shaken.'

(Luke 21:11, 25–26, emphasis added)

Tropical storms whipping up the sea and devastating coastal
regions are increasing in ferocity, something which many scientists
are connecting to climate change caused by global warming. In
Isaiah 24 there is an apocalyptic passage dealing with the destruction caused by overwhelming events in the last days of this age, as
cities are left desolate and their inhabitants scattered:

The earth is also defiled [polluted] *under its inhabitants,*
Because they have transgressed the laws,
Changed the ordinance,
Broken the everlasting covenant.

(Isaiah 24:5)

The prophecies in the Bible warn of the coming time of trouble
in which there will be great heat, trees being burned up and waters
undrinkable as well as violent storms and natural disasters bringing famine, disease and death:

The first angel sounded: And hail and fire followed, mingled with blood,
and they were thrown to the earth. And a third of the trees were burned
up, and all green grass was burned up . . . Then the third angel sounded:
And a great star fell from heaven, burning like a torch, and it fell on a
third of the rivers and on the springs of water. The name of the star is
Wormwood. A third of the waters became wormwood, and many men
died from the water, because it was made bitter.

(Revelation 8:7, 10–11)

Revelation 16 speaks of a time when 'men were scorched with
great heat', when the Euphrates River dries up and there is a 'great
earthquake, such a mighty and great earthquake as had not occurred
since there were men on the earth' (Revelation 16:9, 12, 18).

Looking at what is happening at the present time it is not difficult to see such things coming on the earth in the not too distant future. They are all connected with human mismanagement of the planet and its resources and the coming judgement of God at the second coming of Jesus the Messiah. Following His return the earth will be miraculously replenished and will once again become a fertile and beautiful place, able to sustain the needs of the people during the Millennial reign of Jesus when *'the earth will be full of the knowledge of the glory of the* LORD *as the waters cover the sea'* (Isaiah 11:9).

One thought with which to close this chapter. According to evolution coal and oil were produced by organic waste over millions of years. However, it has been shown in experiments conducted today that oil can be created in a short time from waste products subjected to great pressure. The alternative explanation to evolution is that oil and coal were produced by the effect of the Genesis Flood (Genesis 6–9) when vast quantities of animal life and vegetation were trapped under sediment deposited by the Flood. In this case, coal and oil are the result of the Flood which was an act of God's judgement on the wickedness of the world in Noah's day. Jesus said the conditions on the earth at the time of His second coming would be *'as it was in the days of Noah'* (Luke 17:26–27). Could it be that the material which we have used to build up our modern society is the product of the Flood, the first time God moved in judgement against the whole world? Could that same material be the trigger which sets off the events described in the Bible for the close of this age and judgement coming on the whole world in our time?

Signs of
Social Collapse

6

In the event of a crisis coming on our society, like a sudden cut off of oil from the Middle East causing an economic breakdown or a major terrorist attack or an environmental disaster, how would people behave? Would they stick together and help each other out as the people of the East End of London did during the blitz in the Second World War? Would there be dignified protests drawing attention to social need like the Jarrow March during the Depression in the 1930s? Or would there be a breakdown of society into anarchy with everyone trying to grab what they can for themselves and the weakest going to the wall?

Many people today are already in despair at the way society is going. David Baines, Chief Superintendent of Greater Manchester police force spoke of 'communities terrorised by gangs of feral youths'. He painted a picture of entire neighbourhoods living in fear of the gangs who 'don't give a damn about the police or the criminal justice system'. The newspapers are full of stories showing a breakdown of common human decency in society with mindless acts of violence and destruction taking place everywhere. A child of five taken into a wood by other children who attempt to hang him ... A funeral cortege attacked by a gang of yobs ... Children's gravestones in a cemetery smashed and vandalised ... A teenage girl beaten unconscious by youths who filmed the attack on their mobile phones and then passed it round their mates at school ... A girl of three abducted from her home by three men

As family values collapse there is not much hope that young people will find any guidance from the school. Former teacher Sylvia Thomas went back to teaching after a thirty-year absence. She secretly filmed the chaos she found in the classroom for a documentary filmed on TV. In an article in the *Daily Mail* (25/4/05) she describes examples of the disorder she found there:

> The boys who openly attempted to access hard core sex sites on school computers, the pupils who routinely swore not just at each other but also at me and the scenes of mayhem during which desks were overturned, books torn up and windows smashed. Not to mention the brawls that broke out in the classroom.

She goes on to describe the impossibility of getting the children to be quiet:

> They had their backs to me. The girls were putting on lip gloss. They had mobile phones out, personal stereos, hand held computer games. They were talking, eating, drinking. Despite shouting at the top of my voice I could not get them even to acknowledge my presence.

When she asked them to take out their pens and exercise books she discovered they had brought neither to school with them nor was there any supply in the school. When she asked an eleven-year-old child to be quiet he swore at her. She told him not to talk to her like that. His reply? 'Don't talk to *me* like that – I've got my rights you know.'

The *Daily Telegraph* (23/11/05) featured an article 'Sex lessons – do you know what your children are being taught?' It described the 'Personal, social and health education' (PSHE) lessons in King's Manor school in Shoreham, Sussex. Parents were outraged to find out that lessons for twelve-year-olds taught about anal, oral and digital sex. Moreover, they have virtually no hope of discovering the content of their children's sex education lessons.

Add to all this the influences on people today from TV, computer games, rock music and it is clear that we are moving towards a meltdown of decency and order in society, which when the crunch comes will lead to a time of unique trouble on the face of the earth. If people spend hours of the day watching violence and people acting aggressively towards each other on TV is it surprising if they end up behaving this way themselves? A new broadcasting code brought in by Ofcom states that 'freedom of expression' is its goal and restrictions based on 'taste and decency' have been removed. This will mean a dramatic rise in sex, swearing and violence as anything goes on mainstream TV.

In January 2004 the government downgraded the dangers of cannabis thus encouraging a rise in the use of the drug. However, even those who campaigned for the legalisation of cannabis now recognise that this was a mistake. The enhanced form of cannabis known as skunk used today is up to thirty times stronger than the naturally grown drug. It creates alarming mood swings, causing some who use it to go into uncontrollable rages and exhibit manic tendencies of paranoia, often leading to schizophrenia and mental breakdown. Now the Home Secretary, Charles Clarke, is proposing new guidelines to allow cannabis users to carry enough of the drug to make six joints a day for a year without being touched by the law. This would mean they would not face arrest for carrying drugs with a street value of £1,870, so any dealer caught by the police could claim the drugs are for his own use. Similar guidelines are being given for heroin, crack cocaine and ecstasy.

As well as the drug problem, alcohol abuse is spiralling out of control with an explosion of pubs offering cut price drinks in city centres. As a result, many areas are becoming violent no-go areas for those wanting a quiet night out on Fridays and Saturdays. The government's answer to this is to bring in legislation to open the pubs round the clock, despite warnings from police officers that drunken hooliganism on the streets is stretching their resources to breaking point and hospital accident and emergency departments struggling to cope with sick and injured drunks. One has to wonder whether the politicians who lead our society are deliberately trying to bring us to ruin and to create a situation of chaos so that they can then justify bringing in a police state to control society in the interests of public safety.

It is interesting that in the passage referred to in the previous chapter, Isaiah 24, which speaks of the devastation on the earth at the end of this age, there is a vivid description of the plight of those addicted to drink and partying when the party ends in the calamities which will come at the end of the age:

> *Therefore the curse has devoured the earth*
> *And those who dwell in it are desolate.*
> *Therefore the inhabitants of the earth are burned*
> *And few men are left.*
> *The new wine fails, the vine languishes,*
> *All the merry-hearted sigh.*
> *The mirth of the tambourine ceases,*
> *The noise of the jubilant ends,*
> *The joy of the harp ceases.*
> *They shall not drink wine with a song;*
> *Strong drink is bitter to those who drink it.*
> *The city of confusion is broken down;*
> *Every house is shut up, so that none may go in.*
> *There is a cry for wine in the streets,*
> *All joy is darkened.*
> *The mirth of the land is gone.*
> *In the city desolation is left,*
> *And the gate is stricken with destruction.*

(Isaiah 24:6–12)

If that sounds a bit like a description of New Orleans after Hurricane Katrina hit, it is worth noting that a local pastor called Grant Storms went to New Orleans' Mayor Nagin and his council and told them that they should not allow a 'Festival of Decadence' which was scheduled to take place in the city. He showed video footage of the previous year's festival with gross acts of indecency taking place in public and said that this event would bring God's judgement on the city. He was laughed to scorn and his message rejected. The hurricane came just days before the 'Festival of Decadence' and as a result the same mayor who had rejected the pastor's message was crying out for help to save his drowning city.

All over the Western world today God is mocked and faith is seen as a private hobby for those who need it, but any influence of God is removed from our society. Many people have no idea what the Ten Commandments are, why Jesus died and rose again, what happens after we die. Any ideas they do pick up about God are more likely to relate to re-incarnation or Islam than any teaching of the Bible. Christianity is often caricatured as old-fashioned, narrow-minded and reactionary. You will generally be laughed to scorn today if you say that you believe that God created the world, that Jesus is the unique Saviour or that we will all face God on the Day of Judgement when we die.

All of this has been replaced with a secular humanist world-view which claims to be tolerant but is actually the most intolerant religion imaginable. Today we see many examples of this intolerance. A Christian-run hostel for the homeless in King's Lynn, Norfolk, has been warned it will lose its government grant because grace is said at meal times and the staff put Bibles out for use. The accusation is that it is not 'inclusive' enough of other faiths. A retired Christian couple, Jo and Helen Roberts, were questioned at length by the police after complaining about the council's gay rights campaign. The couple had sent a letter to the council asking if Christian literature could be displayed alongside gay rights leaflets. The officers warned them that their actions were close to a 'hate crime' and sought to 'educate' them out of their belief that homosexual behaviour is wrong. This incident reported in newspapers on 23/12/05 sounds a bit like the way the police-enforced government ideology in the days of the Soviet Union.

The opposition to the Bible comes from secularists who have been campaigning to exclude Christianity from public life over the past thirty years. Back in the 1970s I taught religious education in a large multi-racial comprehensive school in south London. The largest racial group were from the Caribbean and I soon discovered that in general there was far more Christianity in their homes than in the white homes. I taught mainly from the Bible and ran a Christian Union at lunch times. I never had any complaints from the parents of children from ethnic minorities. The opposition came from secular humanist teachers who clearly wanted Christianity out of the classroom. Their reason was that it was not appropriate to give teaching from the Bible in a multi-racial situation. Over the past thirty years this element has gained increasing influence in our society over education, the media, social services, the judiciary and government. They have used the ethnic minorities and the push for multi-culturalism as a cover to stigmatise and eliminate Christianity from our public life.

All of the negative factors mentioned above can be traced back to the abandonment of faith in God and in particular of Christianity in our society. God's order for society is based on the family and the responsibility of parents to care for their children and children to honour their parents.

God tells us to think about *'whatever things are true, whatever things are noble, whatever things are just, whatever things are pure, whatever things are lovely, whatever things are of good report'* (Philippians 4:8), not whatever is degrading and evil. In the days of Noah we read how *'every intent of the thoughts of* [man's] *heart was only evil continually'* and that as a result *'the earth was filled with violence'* (Genesis 6:5, 11). Jesus said that in the last days of this age it would be *'as it was in the days of Noah'* (Luke 17:26). Today, people's imagination is being corrupted leading to acts of violence, by TV, rock music, computer games and drug taking.

The Bible teaches that we are all born with a sinful human nature which causes us to turn away from God and to act selfishly, therefore children need to be taught God's truth and to be disciplined for their own good. Secular humanism teaches that there is no God and no moral absolutes. Today's liberal humanist establishment puts the blame for what is wrong on upbringing, on racism, on the environment, on anything except the person responsible.

Out of this lawlessness we see a society emerging, which is dominated by anti-God values. In Psalm 2 we read of the nations in revolt against God in the last days:

> *Why do the nations rage,*
> *And the people plot a vain thing?*
> *The kings of the earth set themselves,*
> *And the rulers take counsel together,*
> *Against the* LORD *and against His Anointed* [Messiah/Christ],
> *saying,*
> *'Let us break Their bonds in pieces*
> *And cast away Their cords from us.'*

(Psalm 2:1–3)

In other words they are seeking to break out of the restraining influence of biblical morality and do what they like.

This in turn will lead to the emergence of the 'Lawless One' or the Antichrist as the world leader in the last days of this age.

> *For the mystery of lawlessness is already at work; only He who now restrains will do so until He is taken out of the way. And then the lawless one will be revealed, whom the Lord will consume with the breath of His mouth and destroy with the brightness of His coming. The coming of the lawless one is according to the working of Satan, with all power, signs, and lying wonders, and with all unrighteous deception among those who perish, because they did not receive the love of the truth, that they might be saved.*

(2 Thessalonians 2:7–10)

As society breaks down into chaos the end result will be that people in their terror at what is coming on the world will turn to an evil world ruler who will promise peace and safety. However, because he is the embodiment of Satan, he will in fact bring in the ultimate world dictatorship described in Revelation 13.

The Emerging World Government

As the world is falling apart morally, so it is coming together politically. Indeed, many of the problems noted in this book so far are being used by powerful individuals on the world scene to advance the cause of world government. In an address to the UN on December 7th, 1988, Mikhail Gorbachev, then President of the Soviet Union, said, 'World progress is only possible through a search for universal human consensus as we move forward to a new world order.' Since the demise of the Soviet Union and his fall from power in Russia, Gorbachev has been active on the world scene, based in the USA promoting the need for a world government. The number one reason he cites for this is the environment. He contends that a global institution is needed to deal with this global problem, and if we don't act soon, it will be too late – the world will self-destruct. As part of his push for world government, Gorbachev proposes his Earth Charter, a document for which he has become the chief spokesperson and which he believes will save the planet.

On July 20th, 1992, *Time* magazine published an article entitled 'The Birth of the Global Nation' by Strobe Talbott, a friend and former room-mate at Oxford University of then President Clinton, in which he wrote:

> All countries are basically social arrangements. No matter how permanent or even sacred they may seem at any one time, in fact

they are all artificial and temporary. Perhaps national sovereignty wasn't such a great idea after all. But it has taken the events in our own wondrous and terrible century to clinch the case for world government.

Talbott was later appointed by Clinton as number-two man in the US State Department.

In 1996 The United Nations published a 420-page report *Our Global Neighbourhood*, which outlined a plan for 'global governance'. (By 1996 the term 'global governance' had replaced 'New World Order' in such communications.) The UN is the most obvious vehicle to bring in some kind of global government. In December 2001, UN Secretary General, Kofi Annan, gave a speech in Oslo as he received the Nobel Peace Prize on behalf of the UN. He said,

'In the twenty-first century I believe the mission of the United Nations will be defined by a new, more profound, awareness of the sanctity and dignity of every human life, regardless of race or religion. This will require us to look beyond the framework of states, and beneath the surface of nations or communities.'

In other words, states, nations and communities are not able to guarantee human dignity. We are now moving beyond the age of government by states and nations into the age of government by blocs of nations, and ultimately to a kind of world government mediated by the UN.

On 28th July, 2005, Kofi Annan announced an initiative, called the 'Alliance of Civilisations'. The proposal was put forward by Spanish Prime Minister Zapatero and co-sponsored by Turkish Prime Minister Erdogan. According to a statement issued by Annan's spokesman:

The Alliance will aim to address emerging threats emanating from hostile perceptions that foment violence, and to bring about co-operation among various efforts to heal such divisions. The

Alliance is intended as a coalition against such forces, as a movement to advance mutual respect for religious beliefs and traditions, and as a reaffirmation of humankind's increasing interdependence in all areas. These range from the environment to health, from economic and social development to peace and security.

As the threats to the security of nations are all international in their nature, there is certainly a human logic to the idea of creating a global structure to deal with these threats.

Bill Clinton, who is closely associated with the UN and globalist politics, organised a Global Initiative in September 2005 bringing together world leaders from both the public and private sectors to 'come together to make a difference'. The goal is to identify immediate and pragmatic solutions to some of the world's most pressing problems, which Clinton has divided into four themes: how to reduce poverty, using religion as a force for reconciliation and conflict resolution, implementing new business strategies and technologies to combat climate change, and strengthening governance.

Interestingly, the Clinton Global Initiative finds religion to be 'a chief engine of deadly conflict'. Its goal is an 'integrated global community of shared benefits, responsibilities, and values', which raises the question, whose religious 'values' will this 'integrated global community' demand? The advisory board for the Religion Forum is packed with those who are noted for their liberal views toward religion – those for whom dogma is 'problematical'. This means those who believe that Jesus meant it when He said, *'I am the way, the truth, and the life. No one comes to the Father except through Me'* (John 14:6), would be high up on the list of people considered 'problematical' in this new world order.

There are many organisations seeking to bring world governments together – the UN, the G8, the European Union to mention the most obvious ones. In this endeavour, Europe, the continent of the old Roman Empire, is setting the pace. This is not an easy task as has been shown by the problems with the European

Constitution. The Constitution was to pave the way for the EU to become a super state of twenty-five nations with its own currency, flag, parliament, president, foreign policy and legal system that would ultimately replace the individual countries of Europe.

When the leaders of the EU signed up for the Constitution in Rome in October 2004, French President Jacques Chirac told reporters the constitution deepens 'the roots of peace and democracy on our continent'. According to Dutch leader Jan Peter Balkenende, it marked a new chapter in European history giving the continent 'greater capacity for making Europe more secure, more prosperous, more just'.

The 'No' votes on the European Constitution in the referendums in France and Holland in 2005 sent shock waves through the Euro establishment and many felt that these votes killed off the idea of Europe becoming a super-state. However, this is not the case according to Daniel Hannan MEP who wrote in the *Sunday Telegraph* (28/8/05):

> Most of the institutions that the constitution would have authorised are being set up regardless – the European Defence Agency, the External Borders Agency, the Human Rights Institute, the Charter of Fundamental Rights, the European Public Prosecutor, politico-military structures, a collective security clause, a space policy, a diplomatic service. What else does Brussels have to do to shake us out of our complacency? In its refusal to accept the verdicts of the French and Dutch electorates, the EU has demonstrated beyond doubt that it will allow nothing to divert it from deeper integration, neither its own rule book nor the expressed opposition of its peoples. Surely the time has come to admit to ourselves that the EU is set on full amalgamation.

Christopher Booker in the *Daily Mail* (10/12/05) described how the EU has been taking over the powers of our government stealthily with the full permission and encouragement of our own ministers. He describes the EU leaders 'implementing the rejected constitution just as though it were already law'. Examples given are the establishment of the EU's own worldwide diplomatic service, building up its own police force, setting up a European Public Prosecutor, empowering foreign courts to seize documents and search premises on suspicion of offences which are not necessarily a crime under British law. A European space programme has been set up, the European Food Safety Authority based in Italy supervises food and hygiene laws, the Environment Agency enforces laws on pollution and waste derived wholly from Brussels. Powers relating to aviation in the UK have been handed over to the European Aviation Safety Agency based in Cologne, issues relating to railway safety to the EU's Railway Agency based in France and ports and ships are to be regulated by the European Maritime Agency based in Portugal.

Booker concludes:

> We have become the victims of a slow motion coup d'état. Today in many respects the true capital of our country is no longer London. It is Brussels. We are ruled far more than most people yet realise by a system of government which is not elected and which therefore we cannot hold to account or dismiss. In effect we are thus increasingly coming to live in what amounts to a one party state. And the fact that some of our fellow European citizens last summer tried to say 'No' to further integration now begins to look tragically irrelevant. Our one party state marches on, it hopes, for ever.

The prophecies of Daniel and Revelation indicate that at the end of this age there will be a revival of the Roman Empire which will establish a dictatorial government. Chapters 2 and 7 of Daniel are parallel passages in which God gives insight into the world empires, which would follow the Babylonian Empire, which was dominant at the time of Daniel. The fourth empire (Rome) would exist in some form until the second coming of Christ and play a leading role in the last days of this age (Daniel 2:40–44; 7:7–27; Revelation 17:9–10).

The EU has adopted symbols which are very significant in the light of prophecy. The EU flag with twelve stars on a blue background points to the 'Queen of Heaven' and worship of Mary, linking it to Roman Catholicism (Revelation 12:1). Outside the Council of Europe building in Brussels there stands a sculpture of the woman riding the beast (Revelation 17) – a representation of the Greek myth of Europa being carried away by Zeus, the chief of the Greek gods, in the form of a bull. The bull has horns in the form of a crescent, thus combining symbols pointing to Roman Catholicism (the woman) and Islam (the crescent horns). The EU parliament building in Strasbourg is deliberately modelled on Brueghel's painting of the Tower of Babel (Genesis 11; Revelation 17–18). When asked by a secular journalist, 'Why the Tower of Babel?' an EU official replied, 'What they failed to complete 3,000 years ago – we in Europe will finish now.'

It is also significant that European leaders spoke about 'peace' and 'security' as the plus points for the Constitution and the nations surrendering their sovereignty to the EU. The motivating force behind this process is a vain search for 'peace and safety' based on human reasoning and politics, not on faith in the true source of peace and safety, Jesus the Messiah. In 1 Thessalonians 5:3 we read:

> For when they say, 'Peace and safety!' then sudden destruction comes upon them, as labor pains upon a pregnant woman. And they shall not escape.

The EU is a member of the Quartet (USA, EU, Russia and the UN) sponsoring the 'Road Map' to peace in the Middle East. In the event that the main sponsor of this, the USA, becomes less involved, the EU would probably take centre stage in trying to bring about a peace settlement to the region. Already the EU has strong links with the 'peace camp' within Israel and with the Palestinians. Since Israel's withdrawal from Gaza the EU has provided monitors for the crossing point between Gaza and Egypt bringing its forces directly into the Middle East conflict. European Union foreign policy chief Javier Solana said Israel's retreat from

Gaza was a good first step, but one that must be followed by a full and complete withdrawal from the West Bank, including the eastern half of Jerusalem. In an interview with Germany's *Der Speigel*, Solana said,

> Sharon is mistaken if he thinks that withdrawal from Gaza is enough. Europe won't support that. Israel must commit to making the Gaza withdrawal the first step in a process that leads to the pullout from all the occupied areas.

In the last days of this age the Bible prophesies a false peace treaty over the issue of Jerusalem (Isaiah 28:14–22; Daniel 9:26–27) mediated by the *'prince who is to come'* who has some connection to Rome. At this time Jerusalem will be the focal point of world attention (Zechariah 12; Luke 21).

Around the world there is a similar process taking place to what is happening in the EU. Nations are getting together to form regional blocs in order to trade and compete in the modern world. In East Asia, the Gulf region, Australasia, Africa, North and South America, what has happened in Europe is being imitated as the way forward. The 'Club of Rome' also produced a study back in 1972 in which it said,

> The world cannot be viewed as a uniform whole, but must instead be seen as consisting of distinct though disconnected regions. In our study the world system is divided into ten regions.

In Revelation 17:12–13 *'ten kings'* give their power to the Antichrist who becomes world leader.

From the prophetic point of view the most likely place for the Antichrist to arise is out of the European Union. One way this could have happened was through an orderly process via the Constitution and the man being voted into power as President of Europe, but now that looks unlikely. Another way could be through a period of disorder out of which the strong man arises promising *'peace and safety'*. In Daniel 2 we read about the toes of iron and clay of the image which represents a kingdom '*partly strong and partly fragile*' (verse 42), which is by implication unstable.

A number of foreseeable events could cause these strong nations to be willing to surrender their power to a central authority. A Middle East war threatening to cut off oil supplies to the rest of the world, a series of devastating terrorist attacks in major world cities, or even the rapture of the church (1 Thessalonians 4:13–5:11) could cause a global panic as a result of which people are willing to give up national sovereignty and freedom in return for the promise of '*peace and safety*'.

Already politicians and economists are making preparations for a shift in society which would bring the population under the control of a central authority that will take away freedom in order to make people feel safe. The British government has announced measures to bring in ID cards with biometric details embedded in them. Concerns about civil liberties were brushed aside by Peter Hain, leader of the House of Commons: 'If you are bombed by a terrorist, what is your liberty then? In the end people have to be safe to enjoy their liberty.'

Children from Japan to Russia to the United States are being given ID tags so their parents can keep track of them while they are out of the home. *The Times* (2/10/04) reports:

> Tag isn't a game for Tokyo school children. Beneath the flap of Nobuhiko's school bag is a piece of plastic, about the size of a packet of chewing gum. As long as he remains attached to it the tag is his guardian telling his parents where he is throughout the day. Japan has started to tag its school children.

The *New York Times* (17/11/04) carried an article showing how a school in Houston is using ID badges with microchips linked to a computer in a police station control room to monitor exactly where pupils are. Advocates of the technology saw broader possibilities, such as implanting tags under the skin of children to avoid problems with lost or forgotten tags.

The US Food and Drug Administration has given its approval for an implantable chip to be inserted beneath the skin and used for medical records. The company behind the chip, Applied Digital Solutions, pointed to other commercial uses – to identify and track anyone carrying this type of implant. Military bases, federal offices, prisons or nuclear plants were mentioned, to regulate entry to secure locations. Once inside, scanners placed around the site would precisely locate the movements of each individual. There would be no passes, ID cards, or dog-tags, because all the information would be held on the chip lodged invisibly below the skin. If this sounds far-fetched, access to the high-security crime database in Mexico is already being limited to staff who have had a chip implanted (BBC News Online 15/10/04).

Apart from these considerations there is a big push towards a cashless society going on. Some European retailers are already testing schemes that remove cash-handling. German hypermarket Real is working on a cashless operation in which staff scan goods, but customers pay with a credit or debit card at a separate automated pay desk. Philip Robbins-Jones, Tesco's IT strategic development director, said: 'Beyond the next year, we will consider developing a cashless store. The time spent by retailers handling cash is, frankly, embarrassing.' Stung by newspaper reports that Tesco was going cashless, a Tesco spokeswoman said any suggestion it was currently considering cashless stores was 'nonsense'.

However, Sandra Quinn of the UK payments association Apacs said she could understand if stores were considering this option. 'Cash costs retailers money,' she said. 'They have to store it, they have to keep it securely, they have to count it and they have to bank it. So you can see them looking at the options.' Figures from, Apacs, show that plastic payments had last year amounted to £273 billion, beating cash payments for the first time ever. Paul Smee, chief executive of Apacs, said: 'Truly, Britain has become a plastic society. From this point onwards, spending on plastic will always remain ahead of cash.'

A Post Office survey supports this view, revealing that nearly two thirds of twenty-five to thirty-four-year-olds are comfortable using debit or credit cards for purchases costing £10 or less. A third of these also bought items under £5 on their cards. The cashless revolution is spreading wider all the time. London Transport has now brought in the plastic Oyster card which lets its 2.5 million users move around London's transport network thanks to the so-called Prepay feature. This allows commuters to put credit on the card, which uses micro-chip technology, rather than buying individual Tube and bus tickets.

Transport for London (TfL), which runs Oyster, is now planning to develop the Oyster card by persuading retailers to accept what it calls its 'e-purse' or 'contactless smart card'. In this case Oyster customers would be able to go into any of the 2,500 newsagents and other shops where the cards can already be topped up with cash, and use them to pay for inexpensive items such as a pint of milk or a newspaper. On top of this, TfL is looking for major brands to join its network. The Starbucks coffee chain, which has its own pre-paid card system in the US, is understood to be interested in signing up. 'It takes just a fifth of a second to put the transaction through,' says TfL spokeswoman Amanda Brooks. 'People don't have to mess around with change or pay with a credit or debit card.' At the beginning of 2006 TfL announced that it is putting up fares for people using cash, but freezing them or putting them down for people using the Oyster card.

There is a catch with all this. Every transaction we make with cash cannot be traced. Every transaction we make with a credit card is traceable. Every journey made by a commuter using the Oyster card can be tracked. While the clerks at Visa or at the Oyster card HQ may not be interested in what we buy or where we are going, in the event of an emergency or a dictatorship taking power this would mean the authorities could follow you around and monitor your life-style without the need for secret police. Something Hitler and Stalin would have dreamed of! It also means everyone is given a number without which you cannot buy or sell. The problem of course is what if you lose the card, it is stolen or forged or broken? One answer is to put the information on you – in a microchip – and decoded through a scanner.

All this becomes more significant when we read in the book of Revelation:

> *He was granted power to give breath to the image of the beast, that the image of the beast should both speak and cause as many as would not worship the image of the beast to be killed. He causes all, both small and great, rich and poor, free and slave, to receive a mark on their right hand or on their foreheads, and that no one may buy or sell except one who has the mark or the name of the beast, or the number of his name. Here is wisdom. Let him who has understanding calculate the number of the beast, for it is the number of a man: His number is 666.*
>
> (Revelation 13:15–18)

Technology allied to economics and a fear of terrorism and organised crime is making this scenario (which in previous generations sounded like a fantasy) look like a feasible solution to the insecurity people feel in our time. However, the Bible makes it clear that the 'peace and safety' offered by the coming world government will be a delusion and will lead to the tyranny of the beast/Antichrist system and the final war of Armageddon (Revelation 13–19). This will cause the second coming of Messiah when 'the kingdoms of this world' will become 'the kingdom of our Lord and of His Messiah, and He shall reign for ever and ever'. The choice we have to make is whether to put our trust in the empty words of the leaders of the present world system which is doomed to destruction after the brief reign of the Antichrist (three-and-a-half years rising to power, three-and-a-half years in absolute power) or in the words of the Lord who will reign for ever and ever.

As in the Days of Noah

I travel around this country giving talks at Christian meetings on the issues raised in this book. Most people find the subject fascinating, if a little scary, but they also recognise that these things are there in the Bible and therefore of relevance to Bible-believing Christians. Nearly always after such a talk someone comes up to me and says, 'We don't hear anything about this in our church.'

There is a great prejudice against the study of Bible prophecy in many evangelical churches today. In his book *The Purpose Driven Life* (pages 285–6) Rick Warren implies that the study of prophecy is a distraction from sharing our faith. Commenting on Acts 1:6–8, he writes:

> When the disciples wanted to talk about prophecy, Jesus quickly switched the conversation to evangelism. He wanted them to concentrate on their mission to the world. *He said in essence, 'The details of my return are none of your business. What is your business is the mission I have given you. Focus on that!'*

This actually misses the point of the discussion between Jesus and the disciples in Acts 1. Jesus was not saying the details of His return are none of our business, He was simply saying the events surrounding the restoration of the Kingdom to Israel were not going to happen there and then in the lifetime of the disciples, but that they had a job to do, which is to take the Gospel to the ends of the earth.

If the Lord considered the details of His return to be none of our business, it is a bit odd that He should tell the disciples the signs of His second coming in the Olivet Discourse (Matthew 24; Mark 13; Luke 21) and that so much of the Old and New Testament should be taken up with prophecies about this event.

In fact, the idea that there is a conflict between those who want to study prophecy and those who want to get on with the mission of Jesus is a red herring. If you understand prophecy you will realise the urgency of the message of the Gospel going out so that people can be saved from the judgement that is coming on the earth. It is the apostate church that wants to get the Christians away from looking at the end times because the prophecies of the Bible tell us that before Jesus returns there will be false Messiahs and false prophets leading many astray and a false Church allied to the political world system bringing persecution on the true Christians (Matthew 24:5, 23–26; 2 Thessalonians 2; 2 Timothy 3–4; 2 Peter 2; Jude; Revelation 17).

One of the reasons why the message of prophecy is downplayed is that many in the church are being taught an alternative scenario to the one described in this book. Rick Warren has launched a global PEACE plan which aims to enlist 'one billion foot soldiers for the Kingdom of God'. In a talk given to 30,000 people in Anaheim, USA, he announced his plan which 'will permanently change the face of international missions to take on these five "global giants" for which the church can become the ultimate distribution and change agent to overcome Spiritual Emptiness, Self-serving Leadership, Poverty, Disease and Ignorance (or Illiteracy). This is the most important series of messages we've ever taught in twenty-three years here at Saddleback church. We believe it is part of the beginning of a Spiritual Awakening, a Global Movement, a New Reformation. The First Reformation returned us to the message of the original church. It was a reformation of doctrine – what the church BELIEVES. This Second Reformation will return us to the mission of the original church. It will be a reformation of purpose – what the church DOES in the world.'

All of this sounds very inspiring and is having a huge impact on evangelical Christians. However, the idea that the church can change the leadership of the world system and eradicate poverty, disease and ignorance does not square up with the Word of God nor with the reality of what is happening in the world today. Jesus said there are going to be famines, earthquakes, pestilences and disasters hitting the earth with increasing frequency in the last days and widespread persecution of Christians, in fact the complete opposite of what Rick Warren is saying.

This is not to say that Christians should not be involved in giving relief to those in need in the world. But the idea that the church can be mobilised to bring a new leadership to the world which will eradicate poverty and social ills is another restatement of the dominion teaching which has blinded Christians to the truth of the prophetic word over the past thirty years and sent them down the path to disappointment. Dreams of transforming society and endless prophecies of imminent revival always turn to dust and ashes in the face of social reality. More and more people turn to yoga, Tai Chi and other alternative spiritualities based on Hinduism and Eastern religions, Islam becomes more and more assertive, and apostate Church leaders continue to deny the fundamentals of the faith to the applause of the media which for the most part shows hatred and disdain for the Lord Jesus Christ. Meanwhile, crime, violence, terrorism, breakdown of family life and sexual immorality continue to increase at alarming rates across the world, making life almost unbearable for millions.

There is not a shred of evidence either in the Bible or in world events around us that a billion-man evangelical Christian army will lead the world out of darkness into the light of Rick Warren's 'New Reformation'. For a start, there are not a billion evangelical Christians on the earth anyway. The only way you can come up with this figure is if you include the Roman Catholics and other nominal Christians as part of the same church, which appears to be the way of modern evangelical Christianity anyway. Billy Graham said of the late Pope, 'He was one of those rare individuals whose legacy will endure long after he has gone. I will always remember his personal warmth to me and his deep interest in our ministry.' Joel Edwards, Director of UK Evangelical Alliance, said, 'John Paul II was one of the most remarkable Christian leaders of recent times, a Christian pastor with a commitment to evangelisation and the global church and to creedal Christianity.' Brian Houston, founder of Hillsong Church in Australia said, 'We pray that this papacy, like those before it is marked by a commitment to seeing the Christian message go forward and people changed by the power of the Gospel.'

But the papacy has never been committed to seeing people changed by the power of the Gospel. It has controlled them by an alliance with political power and the fear created by a clerical system which denies salvation by faith in Christ alone and adds human traditions and teachings to the Word of God. Historically, Roman Catholicism has not been committed to seeing the spread of the Gospel message, but has persecuted biblical Christianity and prevented the Word of God from being taught.

With this in mind, it is significant that Pope Benedict, in his first Christmas address on December 25th, 2005, urged humanity to unite against terrorism, poverty and environmental blight and called for a 'new world order' to correct economic imbalances.

He said humanity should look to the Christ-child for encouragement in times of difficulty and fear:

> A united humanity will be able to confront the many troubling problems of the present time: from the menace of terrorism to the humiliating poverty in which millions of human beings live, from the proliferation of weapons to the pandemics and the environmental destruction which threatens the future of our planet. Do not fear; put your trust in him! The life-giving power of his light is an incentive for building a new world order based on just ethical and economic relationships.

In his words for the New Year he gave his homily on the
solemnity of Mary the Mother of God. The Church today also
observed World Day of Peace. He said:

> In the face of the situations of injustice and violence that continue
> to oppress different areas of the earth, in the face of the new and
> more insidious threats against peace – terrorism, nihilism and
> fanatic fundamentalism – it is more necessary than ever to work
> together for peace.

He urged all 'individuals and nations, international organisations and world powers' to come together in the cause of peace.
In particular, the pope referred to the United Nations, calling it to
a 'new awareness of its responsibility in the promotion of the
values of justice, solidarity and peace, in a world ever more
marked by the widespread phenomenon of globalization'.

The end-time events which are coming on the world are
bringing about the circumstances in which a one-world system
calling for a new world order in the name of peace and justice,
backed by the UN and the Vatican, will be seen as the only hope
for many people including nominal Christians, both Catholic and
Protestant. As the Protestant and Evangelical churches substitute
the Word of God for experience and hopes of saving the world by
human efforts, so they will become more and more swayed by the
agenda of the apostate church which will find its fulfilment in
the vision of the woman riding the beast in Revelation 17. It is
interesting that the Pope dedicated his New Year message to
Mary, a woman who is held in honour in the New Testament but
nowhere is she worshipped or addressed in prayer. Christians who
know the Bible must come out and be separate from this unholy
alliance, knowing that the only hope for the world is not some
sentimental vision of the 'Christ-child', of prayer to the 'Mother of
God', but a living faith in the risen, ascended and soon coming
Lord Jesus Christ.

In the real Reformation, men like Jan Hus, Latimer, Ridley and
Tyndale gave their lives, being burnt at the stake, in order to bring

the glorious message of the Gospel to people blinded by popish superstition and error. In the mega churches of America which are promoting the New Reformation sponsored by Rick Warren we have dance floors, shopping malls and Christianity made pleasant and palatable to the people, while for the most part the Word of God is left outside, especially when it comes to Bible prophecy.

Much of this kind of Christianity has to be positive. You must only say positive things and never criticise or condemn. But the Bible is full of condemnation of religious leaders who lead people astray and of societies which trample God's law underfoot. The first message given by John the Baptist, the Lord Jesus and the apostles Peter and Paul in the New Testament is *'Repent and believe'*. Repentance means a turning around, a change of thinking from going our own way to going God's way. It implies that there is something wrong with our way of thinking and the direction we are going.

When God looks at our world today He sees so much wrong with it that it is remarkable that judgement has not fallen in much greater measure already. Jesus compared the last days of this age to the days of Noah and the days of Lot (Luke 17:26–32). In the days of Noah we read that:

> The LORD saw that the wickedness of man was great in the earth, and that every intent of the thoughts of his heart was only evil continually ... The earth also was corrupt before God, and the earth was filled with violence.
>
> (Genesis 6:5, 11)

All over the world we see a huge increase in violence at all levels, in the home, in the streets, between communities and between nations. Much of this violence is fuelled by the material with which people feed their imaginations – violent films and TV programmes, drugs and rock music or even religious preachers who incite people to hate in the name of God.

In the days of Lot there was extreme sexual immorality in Sodom with open aggressive homosexuality and gang rape being threatened in the account of Lot's escape from that city (Genesis 19). The sexual revolution of our time has not bought the promised liberation from a repressive morality but a neurotic society, obsessed with sex, but unable to show care and love which God intended to be the bedrock of human relationships. Disease, unwanted and unloved children, depression, insecurity and loneliness are just some of the results of the permissive society.

In both cases there was a catastrophic judgement coming – the flood in Noah's day and the destruction of Sodom and Gomorrah in Lot's day. There was also a way of escape provided from this judgement. In Noah's day the escape was to go into the ark which Noah had built. In Lot's day it was to flee from the city as guided by the angels God sent to warn of the coming destruction.

There was only one way to escape. Suppose someone in Noah's day had thought, 'Well Noah is a bit crazy building a boat in the middle of dry land, but just in case he is right I will build my own boat.' Had he done so he would have drowned. It has been worked out that if you wanted to build a boat which would float in turbulent conditions and did not need to go anywhere, the dimensions of Noah's ark were just perfect. How did Noah know this? God, who was going to send the flood, revealed how to build a boat which would float in the terrible conditions which were coming on the earth. Any other boat would capsize.

In the end-time calamity which is coming on the earth there is only one way to be saved. Jesus said,

> 'I am the way, the truth, and the life. No one comes to the Father except through me.'
>
> (John 14:6)

Peter said of Jesus,

> 'Nor is there salvation in any other, for there is no other name under heaven given among men by which we must be saved.'
>
> (Acts 4.12)

This means that all other religions, cults or philosophies cannot save us in the coming day of judgement. However politically incorrect it may be to say this, other faiths than biblical Christianity will prove as useless as home-made boats in the time of Noah's flood. Nominal Christianity cannot save anyone either. Jesus said, *'Unless one is born again, he cannot see the kingdom of God'* (John 3:3). We must make a personal decision to turn from sin and unbelief towards faith in God through the Messiah Jesus in order to be saved from the judgement that is coming.

The reason for the uniqueness of Jesus is that only He has come from God in the first place, lived a perfect life without sin and borne the sins of the world when He died and rose again from the dead.

According to 2 Peter 2:5 Noah was a *'preacher of righteousness'* meaning that as he was building the ark before the flood he was also explaining to people the reason for the ark and showing them the way of salvation from the coming flood. According to Genesis 19 the angels sent to Lot warned him of the coming destruction of Sodom and told him to get his family out of the place. The text reads:

> So Lot went out and spoke to his sons-in-law, who had married his daughters, and said, 'Get up, get out of this place; for the LORD will destroy this city!' But to his sons-in-law he seemed to be joking.
>
> (Genesis 19:14)

One could say that Noah was a pretty unsuccessful preacher because only eight people listened to him and went into the ark. Lot's sons-in-law thought his warning was a joke and paid no attention. So it is today. A calamity is coming which will sweep away our society like a flood destroying a house built on the sand. It is not just Bible prophecy which is saying this, but those who can see the relevance of today's news reports come to the same conclusion. But still the message of salvation through Jesus the Messiah as the only escape from the trouble that is coming is treated as a big joke by the majority of people in the world today.

The people who scoffed at Noah and Lot's sons-in-law were not

laughing when the calamity came. In the book of Proverbs there is
a remarkable passage on this theme:

> *Wisdom calls aloud outside;*
> *She raises her voice in the open squares.*
> *She cries out in the chief concourses,*
> *At the opening of the gates in the city*
> *She speaks her words:*
> *'How long, you simple ones, will you love simplicity?*
> *For scorners delight in their scorning,*
> *And fools hate knowledge.*
> *Turn at my reproof;*
> *Surely I will pour out my spirit on you;*
> *I will make my words known to you.*
> *Because I have called and you refused,*
> *I have stretched out my hand and no one regarded,*
> *Because you disdained all my counsel,*
> *And would have none of my rebuke,*
> *I also will laugh at your calamity;*
> *I will mock when your terror comes,*
> *When your terror comes like a storm,*
> *And your destruction comes like a whirlwind,*
> *When distress and anguish come upon you.*
> *Then they will call on me, but I will not answer;*
> *They will seek me diligently, but they will not find me.*
> *Because they hated knowledge*
> *And did not choose the fear of the LORD,*
> *They would have none of my counsel*
> *And despised my every rebuke.*
> *Therefore they shall eat the fruit of their own way,*
> *And be filled to the full with their own fancies.*
> *For the turning away of the simple will slay them,*
> *And the complacency of fools will destroy them;*
> *But whoever listens to me will dwell safely,*
> *And be secure, without fear of evil.*

(Proverbs 1:20–33)

If we listen now to what God is saying He will answer us in the day of trouble and take care of us now and for eternity. If we despise and reject His words there is a day coming when He will no longer be able to hear our cry. Now is still the day of grace and it is not too late to call on the name of the Lord and be saved, but do not delay, there is a day coming when it will be too late and those who are outside of God's kingdom will be lost forever.

The Birth Pangs and the Thief in the Night

When will all this happen? The Bible makes it very clear that we cannot know the day or the hour of Jesus' return. In Matthew 24:36 Jesus says,

> 'But of that day and hour no one knows, not even the angels of heaven but My Father only.'

In 1 Thessalonians 5:1–3 Paul writes:

> But concerning the times and the seasons, brethren, you have no need that I should write to you. For you yourselves know perfectly that the day of the Lord so comes as a thief in the night. For when they say, 'Peace and safety!' then sudden destruction comes upon them, as labour pains upon a pregnant woman.

Here we find two very graphic images to describe the return of Jesus. One is to compare it to the birth pangs of a pregnant woman, the other to a thief in the night.

When a woman goes into labour a process begins which will lead to the birth of the child. She knows the signs of the impending birth are taking place, but she does not yet see the child and she does not know how long the process will go on for. Today the signs of the second coming of Jesus Christ are taking place – not just some of them but all of them. We do not know how long it will be before the crisis we are describing in this book explodes across the earth, but there is no doubt that it will. When it does, the world will enter a period of time described in the Bible as the great tribulation. Jesus describes this period in Matthew 24:21–22:

> 'For then there will be great tribulation, such as has not been since the beginning of the world until this time, no, nor ever shall be. And unless those days were shortened, no flesh would be saved; but for the elect's sake those days will be shortened.'

The world situation today is pushing humanity towards an unprecedented crisis in human history which will affect all nations of the earth. This will bring the possibility of the end of all life on earth if God did not step in through the return of Jesus 'shortening' those days and bringing the time of human mismanagement of the planet to an end.

Despite all this there is a glorious hope for the future. Jesus said,

> 'When these things begin to happen, look up and lift up your heads, because your redemption draws near.'
>
> (Luke 21:28)

These things have begun to happen so we should look to the return of the Lord Jesus as the hope for the world. While people without faith are described by Jesus as experiencing heart failure for fear at the things which are coming on the earth (Luke 21:26), the believer has a totally different expectation:

> We should live soberly, righteously, and godly in the present age, looking for the blessed hope and glorious appearing of our great God and Saviour Jesus Christ, who gave Himself for us, that He might redeem us from every lawless deed and purify for Himself His own special people, zealous for good works.'
>
> (Titus 2:12–14)

As the lights go out all over the world, the light of faith and hope in Jesus will never go out in the hearts of those who really believe in Him. In order to escape the coming collapse of oil-based industrial society, Mr Savinar, in the article already quoted, suggests that people should 'relocate to an area as least vulnerable to these issues as possible'. But for many people that will not be a viable option and it will not save you anyway. You can flee from the cities to the empty places of the earth and try to be as self-sufficient as possible, but the coming catastrophe will reach every person and every place on earth. As in the days of Noah there will be no escape.

But the Lord has a plan to relocate His people:

> *For the Lord Himself will descend from heaven with a shout, with the voice of an archangel, and with the trumpet of God. And the dead in Christ will rise first. Then we who are alive and remain shall be caught up together with them in the clouds to meet the Lord in the air. And thus we shall always be with the Lord.*

(1 Thessalonians 4:16–17)

This event, known as the Rapture of the Church, will take place unexpectedly and unannounced like a thief coming in the night. At that moment those who are saved will be taken to to be with the Lord before the judgements fall on the earth in the great tribulation period.

Jesus also describes this event in these words:

> *'But as the days of Noah were, so also will the coming of the Son of Man be. For as in the days before the flood, they were eating and drinking, marrying and giving in marriage, until the day that Noah entered the ark, and did not know until the flood came and took them all away, so also will the coming of the Son of Man be. Then two men will be in the field: one will be taken and the other left. Two women will be grinding at the mill: one will be taken and the other left. Watch therefore, for you do not know what hour your Lord is coming. But know this, that if the master of the house had known what hour the thief would come, he*

would have watched and not allowed his house to be broken into.
Therefore you also be ready, for the Son of Man is coming at an hour you
do not expect.'

(Matthew 24:37–44)

This passage describes a separation, which will take place between those who are taken to be with Jesus and those who are left behind. Whether they are male or female, or outside (in the field) or inside (at the mill), will make no difference. One will be taken and one will be left.

There is a parallel passage in Luke's Gospel, which adds the detail: *'there will be two men in one bed: the one will be taken and the other will be left'* (Luke 17:34). This has nothing to do with homosexuality. What it means is that whether they are awake or asleep will make no difference. One will be taken and one will be left. It is interesting that at any moment in the earth's history on one side of the world it is day where most people will be awake, while on the other side it is night, where most people will be asleep, something the Gospel writers themselves would not have known at the time.

In the light of all this the only hope for the world is the return of the Lord Jesus. Neither political nor religious world leaders are able to save the world, because our modern technological society is a house built on the sand and sooner or later it will come crashing down. God is building a kingdom which cannot be shaken. In the letter to the Hebrews chapter 12 we read:

> *See that you do not refuse Him who speaks. For if they did not escape who refused Him who spoke on earth, much more shall we not escape if we turn away from Him who speaks from heaven, whose voice then shook the earth; but now He has promised, saying, 'Yet once more I shake not only the earth, but also heaven' [Haggai 2:6]. Now this, 'Yet once more,' indicates the removal of those things that are being shaken, as of things that are made, that the things which cannot be shaken may remain. Therefore, since we are receiving a kingdom which cannot be*

> shaken, let us have grace, by which we may serve God acceptably with
> reverence and godly fear. For our God is a consuming fire.
>
> (Hebrews 12:25–29)

The world system today will not stand because it is on the wrong foundations. But when everything else is shaken, God's kingdom cannot be shaken. In order to enter God's kingdom Jesus says, *'You must be born again'* (John 3:7), not physically but spiritually by turning from sin and unbelief to faith in God who raised Jesus from the dead when He had paid the price for our sins by shedding His blood on the cross. Those who believe in Him will be raised up on the last day.

If you have not yet made that step I urge you to do so without delay. Here is a prayer which you can say to accept salvation through Jesus the Messiah.

> Dear heavenly Father, I admit that I am a sinner and need Your forgiveness. I believe that Jesus the Messiah died in my place, shedding His blood to pay for my sins, and that He rose again from the dead to give me eternal life. I am willing right now to repent of my sin and accept Jesus the Messiah as my personal Saviour and Lord. I commit my life to You and ask You to send the Holy Spirit into my life, to fill me and to take control and to help me become the kind of person You want me to be. Thank You Father for loving me. In Jesus' name, Amen.

If you have made a commitment to Jesus already use the time that remains to make the message of salvation known. If you are challenged to do something about this here are some suggestions:

- Pray that God will raise up those who can minister the truth in these days and point people to salvation through faith in the Lord Jesus.
- Distribute leaflets, magazines, books and videos designed to make people aware of the coming of the Lord and the way of salvation (we can supply).

- Organise a Bible study looking at the issues of the end times. (We have produced a series of Bible studies on this subject – The Omega Course, available for £1 including postage.)
- Organise a meeting (in a home or in a church) about the end times and the return of Jesus and invite non-Christians along.
- Study yourself so you are able to show people troubled by what is happening in the world that Jesus is coming again and how to find faith in Him.

About the Author

Tony Pearce leads *The Bridge Christian Fellowship* in Golders Green, north London. He also produces the quarterly magazine, *Light for the Last Days*, giving up to date information on issues relating to the second coming of Christ, and a monthly CD/cassette tape called *This Month in Prophecy*. The magazine is now also available in French, German, Russian, Romanian and Malayalam. Tony has also produced a Bible Study course on the end times called *The Omega Course*.

Tony's other books, *The Omega Files* and *The Messiah Factor*, are available from the address below and from New Wine Ministries, www.newwineministries.co.uk

To receive information on any of the above, please contact:

Tony Pearce
Light for the Last Days
Box BM-4226
London
WC1N 3XX

e-mail: enquiries@lightforthelastdays.co.uk
website: www.lightforthelastdays.co.uk

We hope you enjoyed reading this New Wine book.
For details of other New Wine books
and a range of 2,000 titles from other
Word and Spirit publishers visit our website:
www.newwineministries.co.uk